GOD'S CHILD ON THE RUN

Delivered from the jaws of Kenya's deadly politics

Dearest Kerina Awuor

Grateful for your support always.

You have a heart of gold!

May we live to read your story, some day!

Philadelphia PA, USA

OMWA OMBARA
12/18/2020

Re-sent copy

OMWA OMBARA

GOD'S CHILD ON THE RUN

Delivered from the jaws of Kenya's deadly politics

Also Published by Writers Guild-Kenya

Poetry
1. Through the Journey of Hope Poetry Anthology
2. Lust of My Ink *Patrick Lavince*
3. Desire *Nkirote Kinoti*

Memoirs
4. Nurse on the Run *Christine Kinyua*
5. Dropped to the World, *Adopted by Fate Farhan Yusuf*
6. Unbroken Wings *Nafisa Khanbhai*
7. Diary of the Miaha *Verah Omwocha-Dinda*

Self Help/ Motivational
8. Game On *Kim Chokera*
9. Hey You *Dennis Odeny*
10. Inner Warrior *Jeff Nthiwa*
11. Me vs Me *Kevin Odongo*
12. Questions of My Youth *Gabriel Dinda*

Kiswahili (Riwaya)
13. Ipo Siku *Solomon Muya*

Novels
14. Sins of my Father *Ida Kemunto*
15. Chasing a Bullet *Douglas Logedi*
16. Pains and The Secrets *Mugeni Ojiambo*

Children stories
17. The Kidnappers *Natasha Wambui*
18. Mes Amis/My Friends/Rafiki *Zangu* Elizabeth Wichenje
19. Meine Freunde/My Friends/Rafiki *Zangu Elizabeth Wichenje*

Published by:
Writers Guild Kenya
The Writers Centre, Nairobi.
Email: write@writersguild.co.ke
Website: www.writersguild.co.ke
Phone: +254 751 562 750

This Revised Edition Published: July, 2020

© **Omwa Ombara**

The right of Omwa Ombara to be identified as the author of this work has been asserted by her in accordance with the Copyright, Designs and Patents Act 1988.

No part of this publication may be reproduced, stored in a retrieval system or transmitted in any way by any means; electronic, mechanical, photocopy, recording or otherwise without the express permission of the author and publisher, except for brief quotations in books, articles, publications and reviews as provided in copyright law.

Design, layout, realisation & print coordination by:
Okang'a Ooko @ www.obakunta.co.ke
Cover design by Okang'a Ooko
Oba Kunta Octopus. All Rights Reserved.

ISBN: 978 9914 -9858 -2-5

Printed and bound in the Republic of Kenya

AUTHOR ENDORSEMENT

Omwa Ombara is a resolute pen slinger and a versatile wordsmith who has widely published across the world. She writes across different genres; reportage, feature, poetry, memoir and short fiction. Her writings send the writer into mental jive and usually her poetic reflections jabs through heart caves of the oppressor. She has mastered the art of revolutionary and protest poetry with tact, steed and dexterity. Her poetry cracks truth to double chinned economic mowers and unrepentant fat cats who sleep in parliament while squandering the masses' hard-earned cash, which they loot. Omwa stands firm against dictatorship and abuse of human rights, she is an advocate of press freedom, and fighter of justice for the homeless and refugees. She is a peace-loving dissident using poetry and other revolutionary literature as weapons of instruction. Her pen is a sword of creative defiance. Aluta continua.

— ***Mbizo Chirasha** is a widely published Zimbabwean poet and writer. According to the Stellenbosch Literary Project, "an internationally acclaimed Performance poet, Writer, Creative/Literary Projects Specialist, an Advocate of Girl Child Voices and Literacy Development."*

Acclaim for Omwa Ombara's
God's Child On The Run

A true page-turner. Author Omwa Ombara's story is about how she escaped death during a dark time in Kenya's political history (2007/2008). Intertwined in her story is a unique glimpse into that beautiful traditional Kenyan/Luo culture that she remembers so fondly from her youth. At its core, her story is a reminder about the fragility of the human experience and the rise of the human spirit. It's important to remind the world of these notions. She is so deserving of recognition for her bravery and willingness to risk everything, including her life, in the name of truth and justice.

— Cynthia Hernandez, Attorney, California, US

'God's Child On the Run' is a beautifully written story of resilience and powerful first-hand account from the African diaspora of optimism and redemption. All of us can draw strength from Omwa Ombara's gut-wrenching story, one that only she can tell with such painstaking attention to detail and authentic wit. The story teaches us that there is no moral substitute for true, lived experience. This is a must-read for everyone. It will leave you wanting to embody more of Omwa's tenacity and courage in the face of the seemingly insurmountable adversity. In the end, the walks away renewed and affirmed that we are all on the same journey, trying to find a safe haven for continued personal growth. I recommend this book as a gift for any occasion and perhaps an addition to a monthly book club. There is a lot to talk about and multiple themes to explore.

— Demetris Powell, Attorney, Philadelphia, US

Though I did not purchase this book on Amazon, I felt moved to write a review because of how incredible this story was.

This is an amazingly captivating book, filed with moments that pull you into the story and compel you to ponder, emote, and cheer. I am an American and found this read educational and inspiring as well as thrilling and even terrifying at times. The author does a masterful job pulling you into her journey.
A Thrilling, Heartfelt Story!

— TIFFANY BELL, Program Director, Philadelphia, US

A powerful, intense and captivating book. Meeting Omwa before knowing her story, I had no idea of the horror that she had faced. I am in awe of her strength, tenacity and will to survive life-threatening difficulties. Omwa stood in her truth and after all that she has endured, remains as graceful as her writing. This story had to be told. Thank you Omwa!

— Asha Mollock, Author, The Underground Woman

This book is a powerful and engaging journey that is both harrowing and educational. It's an up close view of how corrupt political systems bring fear, war, and lethal turmoil to a nation. Omwa is a fiercely brave writer who shares her story through beautiful and often heartbreaking imagery. Her unwavering strength can be felt in every word. You won't be disappointed!!!

— NESANEL D.

Omwa Ombara's beautifully written account speaks volumes to those who have become victims of circumstances and targeted for honesty. An innocuous, truthful interview from the past develops into a looming specter, forcing her to flee the country and profession she loves. A must read for journalists and the public at large.

— TOM RHODES, Journalist

Although this is a dramatic experience, it's educational. For those who think journalism is this cushy glamorous career, hold tight. Yes, you get to travel and meet both important and dangerous people; thus, you have to be oh so careful. Who do you trust? Criminals want positive words to describe themselves. If an apple is rotten, it is rotten. Sometimes, your life is not your own. Knowing the truth can put you in grave danger. The story is definitely a page-turner.

— MONIQUE GORDON, author, Binkys Words

Riveting and fast-paced as Omwa, a rare breed of principled but naive Kenyan journalist, determined not to die, hides and flees for her life with her enemies in hot pursuit. It all starts with a single phone call, which turns the quiet life of Omwa into the dangerous unenviable life of an ICC potential witness against powerful dark forces who control loyal, devoted, ruthless thugs, state security, and intelligence. A must read!

— JOAB OKELLO, Attorney, New York

This well-written book gives me a view of a real world that is completely strange to me. Many people have not experienced that dark world or how stark the manmade hell is or can be. Omwa has a unique way with words that gives a colorful description of that life. If you ever read 'The Trial' by Franz Kafka, you will feel a bewilderment of the accused but never will you know what the case was really about, mainly since the accused never knew himself. The book portrays a foggy world seen through a foggy haze of fear and alienation.

— WOLF, computer and information scientist

This highly humorous book is intense, captivating, candid, engaging, inspiring. The author does not dwell on self-pity but draws from her deep well of positive energy to travel the rough corners of her dangerous journey. A must read for anyone who is stuck and wants to move on.

— KORLU EZIKE, medical case manager/therapist

FOREWORD

A CHILLING JOURNEY OF SURVIVAL, TRAUMA AND HAIR-RAISING INCIDENTS FROM A PLACE SHE CALLED HOME FOR OVER FORTY YEARS.

"This story must be told. Let the birds carry it on their beaks and wings as they migrate to distant lands and repeat it upon their return. Let them sing it to the children playing in the fields, that their history may be written in their hearts and not in books edited at political rallies. May the winds that swivel and swirl with force and purpose circulate it all the way from the desert to the sea and from the mountains to the valleys and lakes. Let it be told."

The above words leap out of the introduction of this book that reads like a horror movie with the reader sitting on the edge of a chair, possibly trembling at the truth. For those who lived through the events that, 'God's Child on the Run' detail in the life of this brave woman of letters, a shiver runs down the spine as memories of burnt bodies in holy places, others slaughtered and left on road sides and long lines of displaced people carrying torn mattresses along the highways and familiar roads replay the horrors of a 'land and people gone mad'.

Omwa Ombara had been a journalist and blogger for a while

in the land where her father's bones were interred before the fateful call from a 'Donata' brought a directionless turmoil to her life, media houses of repute can attest to this. The land was ablaze with discontent over alleged 'stolen election results'. Having been a journalist who had extensively covered events and aired dissenting views over the results, the international criminal court in The Hague felt she had something of valued truth to testify in order to bring the perpetrators of the seismic turmoil that had seen deaths, displacement and destruction of property face the consequences of their actions. This call was the beginning of running from phantoms and shadows that trailed her to every place she went. Omwa's words about this phone call, *"By a sudden twist of fate, Donata* turned my whole life upside down like a blind bat sleeping under an old mango tree."* That her phones were tapped and emails hacked was not comforting. Not even when she sought advice from her friends and lawyers on how to proceed with the call amid fears for her life did the feeling recede. *"What you know is just your word against the suspects. Besides, court witness is a full- time job, you know. Are you ready to put your life on hold and be a witness? Remember, some of those international cases have taken up to ten years to complete,"* This was far from reassuring. Nor did the next bit of advice dispel the coldness that was building up in her gut.

"Being a witness is not a joke. It's going to drain you. It's going to disrupt your life. Don't meet them, ignore their calls, anyway, no one can force you to be a witness, it's probably a friend playing a prank on you, it's probably the ICC suspects who want to knock your head off."

And the fear of the unknown and the known hung around this woman whose crime was being a journalist with the truth of the events of bloodshed, looting, burning and wholesale displacement of people from homes they had known for decades and more. That the case in ICC was against the leadership of the country with the means, motive and capacity to silence a dissenting voice, sat coldly at Omwa's heart. She was watched. She was trailed. And soon, she took on the character of the leper where her family, friends and acquaintances had to stay away, some even cutting off communication with her not to share spotlight with the government machinery and telescope honed on her.

God's child had to run to see the sunrise tomorrow. Her tale of boundaries crossed under foggy and grey threats, her arrivals, departures and delayed flights. Her hope and resilience in solitary confinement waiting for gods of justice to study her journey all bring the reader to a place both comforting and uncomfortable. A testimony of the resilience of the human spirit against great odds. A personal foundational in the benevolence of a force beyond the obvious. To Omwa, that force is God, the title of her book bears that testimony.

In this grim tale of political persecution and eventual escape, a box of tissues will come in handy for two reasons. You will laugh at life's fine and fun moments even as you tear over the sorrow of a fugitive on the run.

Omwa's early life affords the reader some beautiful peek at innocence and love. *"I spent my early years around Kisumu town by Lake Victoria. I climbed tall trees to pick up raw mangoes and ripe zambarao, peeped through boreholes for hours, dug up anthills to check out what the termites were up to. I was a mere local girl who attended local churches and schools."*

About her joining university, Omwa had this to share. *"I almost missed a chance to join the school of Journalism at the same University when a neighbour's toddler got hold of my admission letter and played with it outside their door".*

The beautiful heaven of childhood memories, the sad compromising hell of adulthood congregate to give a wonderful treatise on life with all its enrichment and shortcomings.

Omwa's story is a story of many immigrants retelling their past to lend posterity to guard against societal biases that are easily manipulated to cause mayhem, harm, destruction and death by people bent on climbing political ladders at whatever cost. It is the story of bigotry when power gets drunk on its own power, of persecution of those steady in their stand on truths. A story of divisions sowed to keep animosities alive for the benefit of politicians and the hypocrisy of political partisan constitutions, whose underhand deals only owe their egos a social status and immunity to lord it over the population. A story of thinly veiled animosities sold to a people through the tribe and which are activated every election year as Kenya bears witness to events after the tribal clashes drawn by Omwa's experiences and journey since 2007.

Is there hope for this beautiful land that its people will rise against tribal politics and be guided by truth for the betterment of the society as a whole?

Perhaps there is hope.

— ***Nancy Ndeke*** *is a Published Author, Phenomenal Poet and Flash Fiction Writer.*

ACKNOWLEDGEMENT

Due to security reasons and to protect safe houses, witnesses, potential witnesses, and protection officers, some names have been changed. These include workers of: Witness Protection Agency (WPA), Kenya National Commission on Human Rights (KNCHR), United Nations Human Rights Office in Gigiri Nairobi, Kilimani Police Station, the International Criminal Court (ICC) Investigators, and Human Rights Lawyers among others.

This story must be told. Let the birds carry it on their beaks and wings as they migrate to distant lands and repeat it upon their return. Let them sing it to the children playing in the fields, that their history may be written in their hearts and not in books edited at political rallies. May the winds that swivel and swirl with force and purpose circulate it all the way from the desert to the sea and from the mountains to the valleys and lakes. Let it be told.

To my dear Baba (Dad) who watches over us from beyond the grave. To my dear Mama (Mum), who watches over us from this end. To my loving family; my foundation, my pillar, my strength.

To dear family and friends who stuck closer than a brother; Joab Okello (my pro bono Attorney, New York); Linda Damaris, my former colleague at The Standard Group, Kisumu Bureau, who voluntarily typed the manuscript; Clifford A. Williams, my loving husband for supporting me through all those nights I worked with the publisher on edits and re-edits.

To all political journalists in exile who dropped their pen to recoup, lost their voices and their names, who died in vain for doing their job with passion and commitment and to those who risk their lives daily in the cut-throat media rat race as they remain faithful to the call to inform, educate, entertain and protect society. We are like sheep among wolves. My prayers are with you.

To Writers Guild Kenya, for gracefully publishing this edition so that this story may journey back to where it all started – the source.

With gratitude and love, I wish to thank everyone who contributed to the success of this book. God sent you my way according to His timing, timetable, schedule and plan. You held my hand on life's highway when I stumbled on rugged and rocky paths. You brought a smile to my bleeding heart and dried my teary and weary eyes. You risked your lives that I may live as we scuttled through tunnels like hunted mice. It's my turn to save your lives and honour you for your courage so true. The monster must be exposed and slain before it eats us all. The pen is our shield and God our Armour.

Though your names may not be exposed to the world for reasons that the gods have chosen, they will always remain written in my heart and in the good books of our Heavenly father. All the words in this book put together can never repay your kindness, love, trust, humility, goodness, patience, passion, commitment, endurance, honesty and positive energy. Someday, sometime, someplace, bountiful blessings will rain on you and your kin. You will celebrate but may not recall that your good Samaritan deeds in the past attracted these good things. And to those who have, shall more be added and for those who lack, even the little they have shall be taken away from them.

CONTENTS

Foreword .../ i
Acknowledgements ... / ii
Introduction .../ viii

Chapter 1: Something Brewing .../ 1
Chapter 2: Red Hot Lines .../ 14
Chapter 3: In the Twinkle of An Eye .../ 25
Chapter 4: Life On Hold .../ 35
Chapter 5: Unfinished Business .../ 55
Chapter 6: Political Games .../ 61
Chapter 7: Wrong Number .../ 67
Chapter 8: My Family, My Pillar .../ 82
Chapter 9: Back to Square One ... / 94
Chapter 10: Tough Questions .../ 114
Chapter 11: Lemon or Lemonades .../ 128
Chapter 12: No Time to Die .../ 131

Epilogue: Memories of an AFrican Childhood .../ 136
Hidden Agenda .../ 148
In Exile .../ 155

End Notes .../ 158
Author bio .../ 170

INTRODUCTION

The story is set in Nairobi, the capital city of Kenya, a country in East Africa famous for its athletic prowess and unmatched scoops of gold medals in world Olympics Marathons. Kenya is also famous for her political turmoil and difficult politics. Kenya has 42 ethnic communities[2] that speak different languages but are united by two national languages - English and Kiswahili. Her magnificent scenery and wildlife; among them Lions, cheetahs, elephants, leopards, rhinos, buffalos, hippos, crocodiles and the great Mara wildebeest migration places her fame among the seven wonders of the world.

In Kenyan politics, the people must die. Every election year, the politicians make sacrifices to their gods and fresh human blood soils the land. It is written; not in the constitution or the book of life but by political design. They celebrate. Hold homecoming parties. Year in, year out, the cycle is repeated. Until it becomes an ordinary occurrence. My journey from this death bed begins with a call from the International Criminal Court I (ICC also called The Hague). This story is based on a real-life experience. So, help me God.

The year is 2012, on a rainy second day of May and only 15 days prior to the antagonist, Omwa's big birthday bash. The cold Nairobi June season seems to have set in a little earlier this year. Omwa, a veteran local journalist, is going about her normal life when she receives a call from Donata*.

Donata claims she is an International Criminal Court investigator based in The Hague, Netherlands. She says the call is about four Kenyan suspects who are indicted on charges of crimes against humanity.

Omwa is a well-travelled journalist. Her work has landed her in The Netherlands, Germany, Belgium, France, South Africa, Zimbabwe and different parts of East Africa. She has interviewed some of the who's who of the world while on special assignment. Yet this time around, she is not invited to cover the news. The Hague believes she may have crucial information in the coming trials. She is a potential witness. But who is Donata? Is Donata a real Hague investigator or is this a ploy by one of the suspects to knock off Omwa's head or throw her in the dark forest for the wild animals to feast on? Then ethical issues arise. Can a journalist become a witness and quote her sources? Can a journalist change roles, stop covering a story and become the story? The shoe is on the other foot. Omwa becomes the story.

The situation takes a life of her own. Coincidences turn into twists and turns when a few moments later, on her way to meet Donata, strangers on foot and in unmarked cars start trailing her. Her phones are tapped and her e-mail accounts hacked.

Meanwhile, two of The Hague suspects storm the campaign trail as President and Deputy Presidential candidates of Kenya. In their campaign trails, they disparage The Hague and term witnesses, fake. Some witnesses redact their evidence. They allege they were poached and offered goodies worth 30 million Euros each and a comfortable life in Europe. Other witnesses disappear without a trace. Is Omwa a fake witness? Is she even a witness? Will she survive the ordeal unscathed?

CHAPTER ONE

Something Brewing

I WAS NOT A WITNESS AT THE INTERNATIONAL Criminal Court (ICC) at The Hague. I was considered a potential witness.

By a sudden twist of fate, Donata* turned my whole life upside down like a blind bat sleeping under an old mango tree.

Every human effort I made to contact the mysterious Donata*, the alleged Hague investigator, hit a snag. She had initially called my personal mobile and asked to meet me to hold certain "conversations" regarding the now infamous Kenyan 2007/2008 Post Election Violence case. Who was this mysterious woman? Why was it impossible to meet her? Did this Donata truly exist?

After several in-depth consultations with my lawyers in which they cross-examined me, jogged my memory and scrutinised whatever documents I had related to my past coverage, publications or utterances over the Kenyan 2007 December elections and Post Elections Violence, they advised me to keep off. They did not think I had strong enough evidence to be a prosecution witness. I said I would just state what I saw with my two wide-open eyes.

"What you know is just your word against the suspects. Besides, court witness is a full-time job, you know. Are you ready to put your life on hold and be a witness? Remember, some of those international cases have taken up to ten years to complete," they advised.

When the ICC investigator contacted me, I dismissed it as a prank and so did everybody else within my circles. Besides working full time as the Executive Director, Media Liaison and Advocacy Consultants, I freelanced as a contributor of satires and features in local newspapers. Those who knew my plight thought I was simply capitalizing on my high sense of humour to make light of weighty Hague matters.

I spent my early years in Kisumu Town by Lake Victoria. I climbed tall trees to pick raw mangoes and ripe *zambarao*, peeped through bore holes for hours, and dug up anthills to check out what the termites were up to. I was a mere local girl who attended local churches and schools, among them Lake Primary, Kisumu Girls, Ngiya Girls, and Lwak Girls. I then moved to the city, registered at Nyayo House as a private candidate, re-sat my 'A' level exams and joined the University of Nairobi. I almost missed a chance to join the school of Journalism at the same University when a neighbour's toddler got hold of my admission letter and played with it outside their door.

In Kisumu, I often accompanied my then sickly maternal grandma, Nya Sinyolo to the Nyanza Provincial Hospital (Russia). The patients' lines were long and most of them appeared extremely ill. To while away time, grandma and I would sit out on the grass and sing Christian hymns, which she knew by heart. What had I done to solicit such attention from The Hague? What good could come out of Kondele? Who was I to be called by the ICC, the highest court of justice in the land?

"Being a witness is not a joke. It's going to drain you. It's going to disrupt your life. Don't meet them, ignore their calls. Anyway, no one can force you to be a witness, it's probably a friend playing a prank on you, it's probably the ICC suspects who want to knock your head off," – advice, both solicited and unsolicited flew in from left, right and centre, like the gushy floods of River Nyando that breaks its banks every year. River Nyando is one of the major tributaries of Lake Victoria.[3]

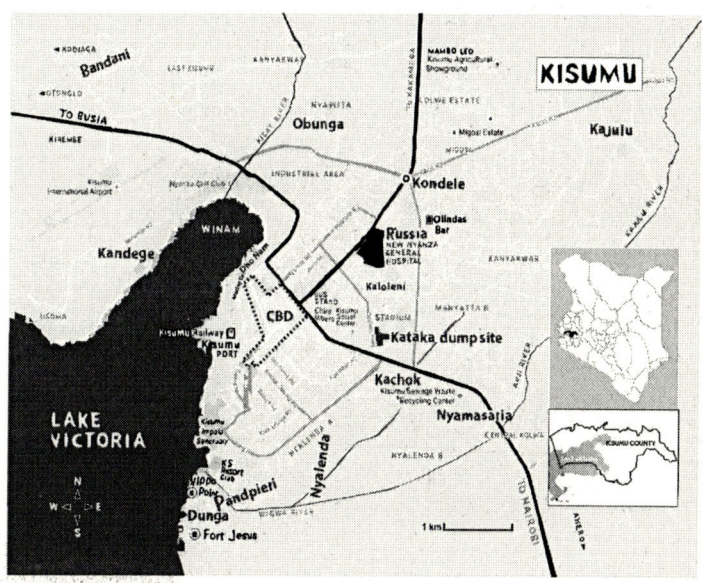

Map courtesy Okang'a Ooko 2020

The Hague seemed to instil deep fear among many Kenyans. Everyone I confided in seemed terrified of it. It was as if contact with The Hague was an ill omen, like the visit of an owl during the day. It was contact with the devil himself, with death. My long-term classmate, friend, managing editor and confidant

Nyaigoti Teitta* warned me: "My dear friend, if The Hague has really called you, I do not envy you at all. Remember, Luis Moreno Ocampo's promise to make the Kenyan case an example to the rest of the world? The best thing to do is to go underground. Disappear for ten years if that is what you must do. Why make a date with the devil himself?"

Although Gambian Prosecutor, Fatou Bensouda took over the Kenyan cases from her predecessor, many Kenyans still identified the ICC with retired prosecutor, Luis Moreno Ocampo. Ocampo, the Argentina-born Hague prosecutor triggered both love and hate in equal measure. He was like an unpredictable passion fruit. Sometimes sour, sometimes sweet.

The drama around the pre-trials, which was televised live on local Kenyan television stations like Kenya Broadcasting Corporation (KBC), Kenya Television Network (KTN) and Nation Television, had reeled the country into shock. Never had Kenya been under such close international scrutiny. Never had Kenyans witnessed the ICC in action. Not once had Kenyans seen their own powerful leaders brought down to size and tried for impunity.

Drama ensued as different witnesses gave conflicting information on the same matter. Kenyan households were addicted to the latest soap opera in town. Only this time it was not written by a Mexican or Nigerian – like most of the movies and soap operas that air on local television channels. It was what the Luo tribe of Kenya call "Agwambo" – something mysterious, beyond comprehension or belief, stranger than fiction, larger than life.

The pre-trial chamber presiding judge; the beautiful, golden haired, prim and proper Ekaterina Trendafilova, captured the imagination of many Kenyan men and many were not ashamed to confess their feelings on Facebook. Some of those who had a "crush" on Ekaterina had said her name meant she was tender and full of love. She looked like a fairy goddess out of this world.

The pre-trial chamber indicted four of the six Kenyans in the list to face full trials. Those who thought the Hague pre-trials were a joke or a movie went into full denial and laughed off the whole matter. But those who knew the sting of The Hague felt the poison trickle in slowly and painfully. Like the sting of a red spider, a bee or a wasp, the red painful swelling was there. Only the blind failed to see it. One of the four indictees, Francis Muthaura, a former Cabinet Secretary and Head of Civil Service, had been acquitted for lack of evidence, leaving three indictees – Uhuru Kenyatta, William Ruto and Joshua Arap Sang.

Although the indictees, their families and friends felt the painful pinch of The Hague's fingers, some Kenyans celebrated the event with equal measure of deep pleasure and malice. Some Kenyans, impressed or inspired by Ocampo's performance in court named their children, dogs, cars, *matatus* and business premises after the prosecutor. They admired him. He was their role model because he had indicted top Kenyan politicians, especially those they had not supported in the last election. Ocampo was their hero.

Like the sting of the wasp, when the truth finally dawned on me that the call was truly from an ICC investigator and that Donata was real, things went haywire. Four Kenyan suspects, were initially committed to stand trial at The Hague on charges of crimes against humanity; persecution, rape, murder and forceful eviction of populations were under investigations. The international investigators were chasing after witnesses as the government tried to stop them and secured anti-witnesses. My blogs and tweets on Facebook and Word Press drew more attention than I imagined especially among those investing The Hague trials and suspects, as Donata would later mention to me in her phone call more than 1300 persons died according to police reports. Media reports said 650,000 were forcefully evicted from their homes. Police reported 350,000 people forcefully evicted. I kept tweeting out these atrocities, sending a message to the world and demanding for justice. I became so passionate about blogging for justice that I soon found myself listed among the ICC's potential witnesses but also at the short end of the stick – targeted for elimination by government forces. Voices of dissent stirring anti-ICC sentiments did not want me alive. They did not just want me silent. They wanted me dead.

Kenyans committed atrocities in 60 days of madness in which the devil took over a community, majority of them being Christians, and steered chaos in outrageous proportions. Forty individuals – majority of them being women and children – who sought refuge were burnt in a church in Kiambaa, forced circumcisions thrived, human and animal heads were chopped off, women and children were raped, and police shot indiscriminately at the public in a spate of politically instigated violence. Even those who had not voted became victims. They had to pay the price of being born into a 'wrong' tribe.

'Wrong' tribe meant different things to different people. It meant you did not share a language or physical territory with a person and therefore you held different beliefs and embraced different values. For those who were circumcised, wrong tribe meant you were not circumcised and therefore too weak and cowardly to lead them. For the uncircumcised, wrong tribe meant you were circumcised and therefore too arrogant and reckless to lead them.

As a journalist, I covered some of the chaos, but mostly in Coast Province and in some parts of Kisumu, my hometown.

Coast Province was on fire with skirmishes, deadly riots and attacks on different communities, especially those that did not belong to the Orange Democratic Party. Mombasa streets that were usually vibrant with international and local tourists, popular loud Taarab music streaming from every store, as if in competition to attract customers bore a deathly silence. Vendors, dressed in white robes and long moslem gowns should have been selling *mshikaki, biriani,* spiced *iliki* tea and *kahawa tungu* (harsh coffee) served in metal baby cups on every corner, as they defied the deadly hot sun. Yet they were nowhere to be seen. What struck one were the remnants of burnt food, pots, molten and charred ashes of plastic chairs, dishes and cutlery. The air was pungent with thick carbon monoxide and burning wood from tyres, tourist kiosks that sold wooden carvings of animals – rhinos, lions, giraffes, elephants, leopards, crocodiles, locally woven baskets *(chondo);* results of chaos of a bungled election.

We saved Tiptip*. Tiptip was one of our political journalists, on the beat for political news in Coastal region. Angry rioters had located his residence a few days back and warned him to leave Mombasa or stay at his own risk. Being a Kenyan from a different tribe made him easy prey for violence, Now they bayed for his blood. We first locked him up in the office. A group of rowdy local youth targeted him as a "foreigner" from a different part of Kenya known as Nairobi. Our office driver, Kibris* was highly experienced in keeping his journalist colleagues safe amid dangerous riots. He was patient, courageous and focused. He often drove us through angry stone-throwing mobs or rioters who burnt tyres to block the highways. He regularly and fearlessly drove through the teargas that clouded the road as we coughed our way through the thick maze of haze to run with the lead story. He ensured Tiptip was safe out of Mombasa headed to Nairobi.

In the midst of all the chaos, I got a call from my Mama in Kisumu. Her voice sounded desperate. She urgently urged me to go home. When I called her back, her phone was off. The automated machine replayed a rough female voice, "Sorry, the mobile subscriber cannot be reached". I panicked. Had a crazy mob attacked her? Was our home on fire? Had they killed my beloved Mama?

I got on to the next Kenya Airways flight from the Jomo Kenyatta International Airport (JKIA) in Mombasa to JKIA, Nairobi but failed to connect to Kisumu. The flights were held up and could not land in Kisumu or Eldoret, a town in the Rift Valley province due to the riots. Along with other passengers, I spent two nights at the airport before I got home, only to find my Mama holed up in the house and she could hardly breathe.

Kisumu city was shrouded in teargas and smoke from burning houses, vehicles and tyres when I arrived. All the water in the vast Lake Victoria would not have cleaned my stinging eyes. It was easier for me to move around with my press card. Angry youth summoned me harshly as they robbed residents along the road in front of Nightingale Hospital in Kondele, Kibos Road. When I flashed out my press card, they let me off with a warning, "report good things about us!" They blocked ambulances that brought in critical patients and would not allow any vehicles to leave the hospital gate. Nurses in blue and white tunics came out of the wards and stood outside the hospital compound. They held themselves, arms crossed against their chests and their faces looked terrified.

In the madness of the moment, some irate youth threatened to burn down the hospital together with the patients and the dead bodies in the mortuary. An angry Dr Chek, a gynaecologist and the proprietor of the hospital, came out to the gate in his white doctor's coat and stethoscope hanging on his chest.

"You will burn the hospital over my dead body!" he warned the crowd. "Onyango, get out of here!" He singled out a former patient at the hospital, whom he had just discharged from the ward a few weeks earlier, now red-eyed.

"Sorry *Daktari*! We are just upset by our stolen election.

These people have messed up with Jakom (pet name for the then presidential candidate, Raila Odinga, by his supporters)! We are good people. We don't mean you any harm." Onyango laughed a little ashamedly. His voice suddenly took a harsh tone. He ordered his fellow rioters to leave the scene. His word seemed law in the group. They hid their crude weapons from view and all followed him into the dingy corridors of the adjacent Manyatta area.

Kondele in Kisumu city was a pathetic ghost town. The *boda boda* cyclists that operated their transport business were gone. Hundreds of women who traded fried fish by the roadside seemed to have vanished into thin air. Thousands of rotten smelly fish lay scattered all over the ground, seemingly abandoned by their owners in a hurry. Everything smelt burnt. Second hand clothes that once hung neatly by the roadsides at Kibuye market were now burnt rags having consumed the fires of chaos of a bungled election. I could not recognise my home at all. The neighbours were gone. A lone, terrified pregnant goat bleated hoarsely as it walked around in circles, confused. Burnt shops, houses and vehicles were a sorry sight to behold.

My Mama's tenant, Mwangi from Nakuru, the cheerful hunchback, who had rented the premises for ten years and become a close family friend was gone, his house raided by strangers, his household goods plundered, the house completely vandalised.

Some residents, mostly Kikuyu and Kisii traders, stayed in tents at the Kondele Police Station. They had been flushed out of their homes as they were believed to have supported the rival Party of National Unity (PNU) headed by President Mwai Kibaki,[4] while over 95 per cent of the locals supported Orange Democratic Movement (ODM) headed by Raila Odinga.

President Kibaki ran for a second term as the President of Kenya. Raila Odinga, son of Kenya's former Vice President

Oginga Odinga, ran as President for the second time.

On my return journey from Kisumu to Mombasa by Kenya Airways, a young woman student, whom I later learnt was called Jane*, a Mass Communication student at a Mombasa Polytechnic confronted me at the Jomo Kenyatta International Airport, Nairobi. Our flight was delayed and we were having lunch at Simba restaurant located on the 5th floor in the transit area, courtesy of the airlines.

"Where are you from?" She asked casually as we munched our meal.

"Kisumu!" I responded. Before I could speak further, her mouth burst into acute verbal diarrhoea. "You must be a Luo. You are the people who threw my sister Mary out of her house in Kisumu and burnt her property! You are very stupid. You plus the whole lot of you! But we're going to show you what we are made of. When we carry out our revenge mission, you will know your place." Her highly charged angry voice spoilt for a fight and I happened to be her first casualty.

Taken aback, I responded softly, "What do you mean? What's the quarrel about now?" I asked her. "We don't even know each other. Why do you attack me like that, my sister?"

"You wait. You just wait until we revenge. You will have nowhere to hide."

"Now, what have I done to this lady?" I asked as I threw my hands up in the air. Other passengers watched the drama in discomfort. They shifted nervously in their seats. It was obvious they were uncomfortable with what was going on but did not want to take any sides. It was that dark moment in the history of Kenya, when no one wanted their tribe known for fear of being attacked, that dark fearful season when Kenyans spoke in whispers as if every wall had ears. Post-election violence was on and exposing one's tribe was anathema; it could cost you your life!

"Shut up and go to hell you uncircumcised people! I am not your sister. I am a Kikuyu and you are Luo! You will know what it means to play around with circumcised people, you piece of rubbish. Why did you burn my sister's house? Why did you make her suffer? Why did you throw stones at her? Do you know that she is injured?"

She got up and charged at me with her knife and fork like an angry buffalo, at the foot of God Jope hills in Migori, Nyanza. "You will pay for what you have done to my sister!" she shouted.

Words hurt more painfully than sticks, says Lawino, the protagonist in Ugandan writer Okot P'Bitek's poetry book, "Song of Lawino". Jane's words hurt me deeply. I did not like to be judged by my tribe and its culture. Luos do not circumcise their people, I was not circumcised. I was a unique individual created in the image of God. I had talents or gifts I had been created with, or acquired which I dreamt would make a better world whenever I had a chance to use them. Yet in Jane's eyes and those of a lot of other Kenyans, with whom I did not share a tribe, a skin or customs, I was useless. I was from the 'wrong' tribe. Jane made me feel as if a sharp knife had been dug deep inside my self-esteem. I got on the defensive.

As I jumped backwards to evade her attack, three male Asian passengers with turbans, sitting on either side of us dashed and surrounded her, blocking her from me. One held up her hand in mid-air and blocked her from striking me with a blow. I do not know how deadly Jane's blow would have been or how many teeth I would have lost because she never got to do it. I was disturbed, disoriented, disillusioned.

The Asian passengers had come from Miwani Sugar Mills, about 15-minute drive from Kisumu, where they had gone to strike a deal on how to buy the Sugar Factory that was under receivership, I had gathered from their earlier conversation. The Nyanza sugar belt stretches from Songhor, Koru, Fort Ternan,

Chemelil, Awasi, Ahero, Miwani, and Kibos to Awendo and Kisii to the south.

Meanwhile, one other passenger dashed for the Manager of the Restaurant.

"I am a journalist and I just went to check on my mother who is ill. I don't live in Kisumu and I did not burn your sister's house! I don't know why you just attacked me for nothing," I raised my voice at her, now really furious.

"Please, please, Madam, cool down! There is no need to fight. You are all sisters, Kenyans. Just be friends, you know!" all the passengers pleaded at the same time.

"What a shameless creature! How can you even dare say you are a journalism student? You lack the qualities of a journalist. How will you make it as a reporter when you are so emotional, biased, unobjectively temperamental, and so grossly tribalistic? What if you ever show up at a media office for an interview and found I was your new boss? Think far ahead, my dear sister. Take a grip of yourself! We are both Kenyans, please!" I told her. I tried to restrain my anger.

She was young, about 23 and I looked at her like a younger incorrigible sister.

Jane looked down, slightly ashamed. She mumbled something under her breath in her mother tongue, picked her knife and fork and started eating again.

The manager arrived a few minutes later after the drama. After listening to both sides of the story, he asked us to keep cool. He did not want to take sides. I could not tell whether he was from my tribe or Jane's tribe.

"If you two continue with your altercation then I will have to drop you from the passenger list to Mombasa and replace you!" he warned.

The flight from Nairobi to Mombasa was about 40 minutes. While up in the cloudy sky, Jane Kamau walked down the aisle and shyly smiled at me.

"I am sorry my sister, I got carried away but you see I am very angry with your people!" she explained as she apologised. "I really didn't mean to hurt you, but I am really upset with your people."

"It's okay," I said, eager to make up with her, "I am sorry I was rude to you too. I love you!" I apologised.

I understood her pain. The atrocities that were committed against her sister and many other Kenyans were horrendous and should not have happened to anyone, irrespective of their tribe or lot in society.

Still, when we alighted, I avoided Jane like the plague and did not look back. I jumped into a taxi and headed off to my house in Ganjoni -- just a five-minute drive from my office. Still, the incident left a bad taste in my mouth and when the revenge finally came a few days later, it was just as Jane had promised and prophesied - heartless, deathly, devastating. Kenya was on fire. Emotions prevailed over reason. Acts of lawlessness and impunity prevailed.

Even before I met the investigators, strangers began to follow me. My telephone was blocked and my emails hacked. I knew my life was in danger. I contacted the Committee to Protect Journalists, the Kenya National Commission on Human Rights, the UN Human Rights Office in Gigiri, Nairobi and the Witness Protection Agency. I went on the run.

CHAPTER TWO

Red Lines

WHEN THE HAGUE COMES CALLING, Beware! Life Will Never Be the Same Again.

I have faced many deaths before like the proverbial cat with many lives. Yet none had created fear in me as the death threats related to the Kenyan post-election violence. Two telephone conversations will never leave my mind, till death. The first one was from a Member of Parliament, now ICC indictee and Deputy President of Kenya, Mr William Samoei Ruto[5] way back in 2007, before the chaotic Kenyan Post Election Violence.

The second one was from an International Criminal Court investigator, whom I will call "Donata", on May 2, 2012 at 12.30 pm. She asked to meet me. At some point in the map of life, the first and the second calls connected five years later and together forced their way into my life's doorstep and let themselves in.

The first call was to do with the infamous "brown envelope" that remains an open secret among journalists all over Kenya. The brown envelope is a term used in media to express gifts that are given to journalists to cover events favourably. This practice is particularly institutionalised by Public Relations officers in government offices whose job is to give a positive image of their organisations. Government offices in Kenya use brown envelopes to circulate or post their official envelopes. Their PR officers, therefore, use the same envelopes to place a little money to distribute to journalists for their "lunch" or "transport". From the government side, it is meant to be a gesture of goodwill or appreciation to journalists for taking their time to cover the event.

However, media ethics does not allow journalists to accept any form of gifts, whether freebies or cash as they are simply doing their job and they are paid a salary or wage for it. The brown envelope has often been abused by some journalists who make specific demands for what gift they should be given and even blackmail individuals and organisations to pay them for coverage. Some politicians also use the brown envelope to bribe reporters and editors to have their stories run on page one of the newspapers. I was allergic to the "brown envelope" and would not touch it even if you put a gun to my head.

When I witnessed the then Eldoret North Member of Parliament and his aide distribute the brown envelope to journalists at an ODM rally I attended in Kilifi, Coast Province, my feelers went on the alert. I had been transferred from our Nairobi office to the Mombasa Bureau to straighten up corruption in the office and I was not going to fall victim to this.

"It is no easy task, Omwa," my Managing Editor, Chris* warned me as he gave me tips to use at my new post.

"It is going to be a tough call but we believe in you as a company. I know you are strong and forthright. I know you are not afraid of anything. You will make it." he said and wished me good luck.

The 2007 presidential election campaign was at its peak in Mombasa. The campaigns were approaching the last leg. Party of National Unity (PNU), led by President Mwai Kibaki, and Orange Democratic Movement, led by then Langata MP, Raila

Odinga tried to outdo one another. They acted like jealous wives in a polygamous home competing for the husband's attention, each out to make the best dish to monopolise their way into the man's heart.

ODM harped on how a greedy tribe of hyenas had ruled Kenya for too long and it was now time to "remove all the '*madoadoa*'" (spots) and dump them in the sea.

"A Tsunami is coming! There it is. I can see it. It is gathering clouds. It will rain cats and dogs. It will collect all the *taka taka* (rubbish) and throw it into the sea!" Raila prophesied. *Madoadoa*, within the original context of Raila's speech, meant that ODM voters should vote in a three-piece pattern for President, Member of Parliament and Councillor.

"It does not make sense to have an ODM President and a PNU MP from the same region. That will weaken our votes in Parliament," he explained. PNU on the other hand harped on how uncircumcised men from a community of stone-throwers could not be leaders. President Kibaki was going around everywhere in the country, often referring to his opponents as *"mavi ya kuku"* (chicken droppings), much to the delight of his supporters.

"They call us uncircumcised and yet we marry their women," some ODM politicians mocked their rivals at the rallies.

"How do you know Raila is not circumcised? What do you want with his organs, unless you are homosexual and you want to marry him? The only person who knows whether Raila is circumcised or not is his wife Ida. And she has not complained. So why are others complaining?" Raila asked at several rallies as crowds of his supporters laughed and clapped their hands in approval.

Although the jokes made at the various rallies seemed innocent and entertaining, seeds of discord were sowed and they would later germinate into what became hate speech. Stereotypes and prejudices soon sounded like facts and incitements charged the population for violence.

First Lady Lucy Kibaki in whirlwind speed and military chopper proudly touted her husband as a very intelligent, handsome, family man and the first African to get a First-Class degree in Economics from the prestigious Makerere University in Uganda.

"I have tested and tried him. Makerere University has tested and tried him. And the answer is an 'A'. What else do you want?" And the fervent, highly politically charged crowd danced, waved and sang in response; *"Ndio maana tunasema aendelee! Ndio maana tunasema aendelee!"* (That is why we endorse him to continue his term).

It was obvious that Lucy had great oratory skills and envious control of her crowd. The women loved her. She seemed to have a connection with them. She seemed to understand their needs. After each rally, women – most of them young mothers, some teenagers with babies tied on their backs – assembled in the halls where they were each given a pair of *kangas* and two kilograms of sugar.

"Mama Lucy's PNU is rich in finances while ODM is rich in words. Words are sweet but they cannot feed an empty stomach. ODM is a hub of entertainment but they are short on funds. *"Kwa ODM tuna kula vicheko kweli, lakini kwa PNU twashiba njaa!"* (We really laugh at ODM rallies but we get to satisfy our bellies in PNU rallies), one talkative woman announced as she packed her sugar into her grass woven basket. *"Kweli hilo ni kweli,"* (That's true,) they responded.

The "Pentagon Wives" comprising Ida Odinga, Rachel Ruto and Mrs Najaah Balala[5] snaked their way through the rough roads of Kinango and Kilifi in praise of their husbands. They stopped by hospitals and Ida named two newborn babies – Ida and Raila. And at rallies they sang, *"Wamama msilale, lale, lale,*

Wamama msilale, bado mapambano, mapambano, mapambano!" (Mothers, don't you slumber, the fight is on).

Hungry, frail, thin-looking women attended the rallies. They had scrounged for food and dug the dry barren soil with their bare hands, eaten poisonous weeds and barely survived. Many had walked tens of kilometres to the rally, their sunken eyes a well of hope. They listened hungrily, expectantly. Their deep-socketed eyes stared tiredly at the well- adorned political wives. But no hand-outs came. They left the rally with empty hands.

As the Coast Bureau Chief /Provincial News Editor of The Standard Group, I could do nothing about other journalists. But I could do something about two of our reporters who accepted the "bribe", or so I thought. I suspended them from work and demanded that they return the brown envelopes if they wished to keep their jobs.

The suspensions caused such a furore within the media and political circles as never experienced before in the history of the Kenyan media. The Orange Democratic Party politicians asked why I wanted to spoil their party. They alleged that they were doing quite well on the campaign trail and any media reports that exposed them as corrupt would hurt their image and cost them the elections.

Politicians at the rallies inquired who I thought I was to deny poor journalists a chance to make money. I had touched a raw nerve and caused turbulence in the calm and silent corrupt media and political waters. Colleagues saw me as a traitor who had blown the whistle on a generally accepted practice.

At the various ODM rallies at the Coast, sometimes attended by more than 60 MPs at one sitting, from Taita/Taveta then to Kilifi, Kwale, Malindi, Mombasa, to Lamu, politicians disparaged me publicly. They did not understand our need to suspend our journalists from work for taking bribes yet we did not pay them well.

"We keep these journalists alive, don't we? Your media houses do not pay your correspondents for several months and then you suspend them from work when we sympathise with them. That is why they beg us for money! Without our brown envelopes, they would die from starvation!" they told an excited crowd who danced and cheered them on. The politicians seemed to know all the on-goings in the media houses. Their moles amongst us who updated them on in-house matters from what they were paid, who earned what, what had been discussed in staff meetings and what would be published the following day, did quite a good job.

One of my bosses in Nairobi asked me to go slow on the matter and recall the suspended journalists back to work.

Journalists were not the only ones who took bribes. Many politicians did it as well. It seemed an established part of some political careers to bribe voters during elections. Some voters held politicians at ransom by demanding money. The Kshs50 denomination note became a bribery signature for politicians criss-crossing the country in search of votes. I witnessed politicians walk around with Kshs50 notes and distribute them to a long queue of voters. The voting period had been nicknamed the Kshs50 season. Sometimes, politicians did it openly, other times discreetly. Some used their agents to do their dirty jobs.

Some journalists went overboard with their brown envelope mastery. I recall a meeting I had with the then Coast Provincial Police Officer (PPO) King'ori Mwangi at the Police Headquarters in Mombasa. His concern was that journalists were very hungry. He alleged that some journalists at the Coast sometimes went to his house and ravaged food from his refrigerator.

"You need to hold a tight grip of your journalists. They seem very hungry. Please try and pay them. I don't want them eating everything in my house again," King'ori said, laughing. I did not find that funny. I was speechless.

King'ori reiterated, in a fatherly voice, as if he understood the plight of some very hungry children.

"They are hungry. Your reporters are hungry. Please try and do something about it because their behaviour really undermines the image of your newspapers."

When I later asked our reporters if they knew anything about their ravaging of King'ori's fridge, they laughed hysterically.

"Leave King'ori alone, Mama," one of them said and they both burst out laughing again. The staff called me "Mama" out of respect, a custom used to address women at the Coast. I was embarrassed but I could not help the situation. It is a fact that reporters, especially correspondents, are paid poorly and often late. Sometimes the money would come after three or four months. Most are paid per story except for those who were on retainer. Their payment was a policy matter over which I had no say. The reason I specifically mention Mr. Ruto over the brown envelope, although many of his political colleagues practised the same culture, is that I got directly involved with him in a situation. The situation is what led to this story and the reason why The Hague investigator approached me.

It was one late afternoon in Kilifi, Coast Province, and the campaigns were approaching their peak. Eldoret North MP and member of the Orange Pentagon – the supreme ODM party organ comprised of five regional representatives – had called a rally in Kilifi town. Crowds milled and danced as they awaited his arrival.

A few minutes before the rally ended, about 4.30pm, as Mr. Ruto gave his speech, I watched a group of excited journalists from all the media houses at the Coast gather under a coconut tree. They looked like children about to receive their Christmas gifts. One of Ruto's aides walked around with an empty foolscap and a blue Bic biro pen. He listed names of reporters and cameramen from the different media houses. One Journalist, Frank*, helped him out with the names. I sat next to the platform and keenly watched the aide. He went to Ruto and gave him the list. Ruto looked at it briefly. He dipped his right hand inside the left side of his brown sweater and pulled out a wad of notes tied in a brown rubber band. The notes looked new and smelled fresh, like they had just been printed.

When I saw what happened, I demanded to see the list. I saw my name on it somewhere down at number eight out of 12 and demanded that it be deleted at once.

"What list is that? Who put my name on that list? Did you ask me? "I asked the aide and the reporter who was his accomplice.

"Don't shout at me!" the reporter told me off. "I don't work for you. I am not from your media house. What I do here is none of your business!" he retorted. He was defiant and very red-eyed, hungry for money.

"Yes, that's true. It is none of my business. So why did you make it my business by putting my name in a corrupt list?" I probed.

I threw tantrums and screamed that I wanted my named deleted as fast as possible from the wretched list of corrupt journalists. The Aide pulled aside some reporters and whispered something in their ears. They went and got into our staff car.

After he distributed Kshs 2000 to each reporter from the other media houses, The Aide followed reporters and got into our staff car. He tried to dish out the money as quickly as possible but I caught him in the act. Colleagues, caught with their hands in the sugar jar, tried to hide the money by throwing it on the floor of the car and stepping on it.

No one is allowed in the company car save for members of staff. I wondered where The Aide got the audacity to enter the car and sit on my seat. I asked what The Aide was doing in my seat but answers were non-committal.

"Did you take the money too?" I asked the driver. He shuffled uncomfortably on his seat but did not respond. He would not look me in the eye.

"What are you doing in our official car"? I asked The Aide. He smiled slyly.

"Relax madam. Just chatting up these friends of mine," he said.

I asked those reporters who had taken the money to return it to Mr Ruto. I warned them of dire consequences. They said they would not do so. When we got to the office, I suspended those involved.

A few days after the incident in Kilifi, a senior politician called me on my personal mobile phone. Just like The Hague investigator years later, I had not met him before and I had not given him my number but somehow, he had it. I suspected he got it from one of the reporters in my office or a source. We had what I thought was a strange conversation. His voice sounded smooth, oily, friendly, cunning and manipulative – a master orator. The conversation took about ten minutes.

"This is *Mheshimiwa*." He introduced himself. He went around in circles, and then finally came to the point.

"Now, Madam, we did not give reporters any bribe," he insisted. "This is a figment of your own imagination. Why don't we forget this small matter so that you can recall these young people back to work?" he laughed forcefully.

"You did!" I insisted relentlessly. "I saw it with my own

eyes. And the next time you try such a thing with journalists, *Mheshimiwa*, I will expose you as the most corrupt politician in this country!"

He seemed slightly taken aback. He paused and quickly recovered.

"If you admit that you bribed them, I will recall them and we shall forget the whole matter. It all depends on you, Sir! I also demand an apology from you for your poor behaviour!" I told him politely.

Mheshimiwa was adamant. "This is going to be very bad for our campaigns," he said quietly, his voice now subdued. "I did not bribe those reporters," he repeated.

"Between you and me, you know very well that you bribed them. But for their own sake, I will recall them," I said. He laughed and hung up.

This telephone conversation left a bad taste in my mouth. I wondered whether *Mheshimiwa* had a conscience, especially if he could blatantly deny what he had done in public.

When an investigative journalist, Safari* visited my Mombasa office with an assignment from a Nairobi Governance Center and asked for an interview over the incident as it related to corruption in the media, I agreed. He said he would interview all media houses in Kenya about the untamed corruption among its reporters and editors, narrowing down to politicians and government bodies. I had not heard of the Non-Profit before, but Safari was a reputable journalist and an old colleague. In the interview, I discussed with Safari the different forms of corruption I had experienced ranging from corruption at the Kenya National Examination Council, the sports industry, the Water Board and the Ruto incident.

This story was published in a local journal, "Expression Today".

A call from the ICC

Donata called me up on my personal mobile five years after Ruto's call. The boil that I had long thought was dried up and healed suddenly surged forward, swelled, burst wide open and bled furiously. My life was in danger. I fought the urge to stay and fight. Then I remembered my late grandmother Nyandwara's wise words - *"otoyo moluor ema ru"* (The cowardly hyena gets to see a new day). I went on the run and lived to tell the story.

CHAPTER THREE

In the Twinkle of an Eye

Life can change in a second, in the twinkle of an eye. It can change with death in the family, the loss of a job, the stroke of a pen, a broken relationship or a mere insect bite. It can change with a slip on the bathroom floor or on a carelessly thrown banana peel, a car crash or a visit to the doctor – and a cancer diagnosis. Life can change with a kiss; it could be the kiss of life or death. It can change with one word spoken as the truth. It can change with Post Election Violence and the eviction of an individual from their homes. It can change for a potential or actual court witness when threats come and forceful disappearances occur.

Sometimes, the gods may be angry when they pay that surprise visit. Sometimes, they may be harbingers of good news. Woe unto you, when the gods visit to settle an old score. That is what happened when the gods appeared in Woodley Estate, Nairobi, where I lived.

The change came to me like a thief in the night; it came in the form of a phone call at around midday. The call from *Donata who claimed to be an ICC investigator, a lady I thought was kind, gentle and friendly, changed my life forever.

Initially, she acted like a humble, understanding, endearing lady. But after a series of events, I gave her a straight No! Not when her good manners and integrity later came tumbling down like the walls of Jericho. Not when she denied that she had ever approached me, made me lose credibility among my family, friends and colleagues. Not when her voice of reason later fell into little cracked pieces like grandma's earthen pot that had fallen as I fetched water from River Oroba, in the Kano plains of Lake Victoria - at the foot of the Nandi Hills. River Oroba is a tributary of River Nyando in the vast shores of Lake Victoria, in Nyanza Province. Oroba falls on the leeward side of the hills. There lies my ancestral home.

Why, you may ask, do I compare Donata to a broken pot?

It was during one of those precious holiday visits to my grandmother, Nyandwara; a proud, tall, dark, and slim woman who often praised herself. She said she was as beautiful as a stamp on the back of an envelope, ready to be posted to the owner at the local post office – "the beauty of an envelope is in the stamp," she claimed. I still remember her in her favourite long blue nylon dress and matching headscarf which she wore every day, despite my Baba buying her clothing from "Deacons" in Kisumu.

She folded them neatly and kept them safely in her huge black trunk. And when she died, I watched in amazement as female relatives fought over her clothes, a few days after her burial. It was a part of our Luo culture to distribute a dead relative's clothes – in memory of the deceased.

After my brief encounter with Donata, I knew I would soon be dead and buried and relatives would distribute my clothing. I really did not mind if relatives shared out my clothing. I had piles of clothes and shoes in my wardrobe, which I had not worn for years. What I did mind, was to die at a time when I was busy and had great plans for my future. Why die when life was so sweet? My Belgian man-friend and trusted companion Wolf* and I were in love when the gods invaded my life. We had made a commitment to spend our lives together and he was about to visit me in Kenya from Belgium in the following two weeks. Poor Wolf and I. Donata messed up our plans.

Nyandwara stood for the truth always, without fear or favour. She had no time for niceties. She called a spade a spade and not a big spoon. My Baba had taken after her but he was often more discreet. When Nyandwara saw a fat woman she would immediately comment, "Wonder of wonders," she would shout, ensuring the woman heard her, "What greed?" she said. On the other hand, when she met a skinny woman, she would ask her directly, "Wonder of wonders, why are you so thin? Are you that much frustrated? Are you in an unhappy marriage? Have you no food to eat?"

Perhaps it was her unique way to show concern but she left many people offended. Perhaps it was this candid character that I had inherited from her, a character that would put me in serious trouble - the path of truth that led me to Donata.

River Oroba, a tributary of River Nyando is only half an hour's drive from Kisumu town where I was born.

Kondele was a village then with only a few families. There were only two tarmacked roads – Kisumu-Kibos and Kisumu-Kakamega roads while the rest were footpaths, until the present town came and forced itself onto the village. Mrs Sarah Ondele was a kind soul and a land owner. She invited her relatives and together with her husband John, gave them free land or sold it to them cheaply. Mama Sarah thought it wise to have relatives as neighbours than to have friends whose neighbourliness had not yet been tested and tried.

I went to Lake Primary School, next to the Kisumu Bus Stop, at the Jubilee market. The school is a ten-minute walk from Lake Victoria. It is also a ten-minute walk from Kondele. As children, we ran to school in the morning, ran home for lunch, ran back in the afternoon and ran back home after school. There were no *matatus*, *bodaboda*, bicycles, *tuktuks* or motorcycles. Few people owned cars at the time.

The environment was quiet and peaceful, close to town yet far in character with occasional music streaming from bars like Dasarile and Casanova, and the *Busaa* clubs scattered in the area. It was whispered that Nyamwaya Kwesi, a famous Kisumu tycoon, had named Dasarile bar after his four wives – Damaris, Sarah, Risper and Leah, thus Dasarile. Polygamy was a highly-respected culture and the more wives one had the more influence one had in society. It was a sign of good financial acumen, potential leadership and good taste for the female species. Owning a bicycle then was a great privilege akin to owning a Mercedes Benz or an airplane today.

When school closed, the most precious moment was a trip to Kabar, to Nyandwara's home. She welcomed us with a fond, sincere grandmotherly smile, with delicious cold millet porridge and *nyoyo* (boiled maize and beans), always stored in a huge dark pot in her bedroom. She kept several earthen pots and a small one for me to use for fetching water from Oroba, whenever we visited her. Nyandwara or "Buko" as we sometimes called her was not easy to impress, but if you did, she would reward you lavishly. She would prepare a whole chicken and serve it all to you as other children and adults watched enviously.

No wonder we all went overboard to impress her. Of course, it was not possible for an eight-year-old to 'demolish' a whole chicken but that was not a problem. Sometimes it was *kamongo* (catfish) specially prepared with a granny's culinary expertise. Fish was the main dish as it was easily available from Lake Victoria and from its many tributaries, among them Oroba. During the rains, Kabar flooded and lots of fish would find their way into granny's cold hut.

There was tilapia, *mumi, sire, fulu* but nowhere to cook it as the earthen cooking place was wet and the firewood dripped with water. The floods were awful and even the birds were sad. The trees had been uprooted and carried away with their nests. They flew sadly from one place to another and sang:

Winyo ywak ni tho,
Apiyo otho pi onego
Nyithindo nonywolo tara,
nyithindo otho pi onego.

(The birds wail, they are dying,
Apiyo is dead, killed by the floods.
She had many children,
the children died from the floods).

When the rains ended, it was awfully dry.

My cousins and I fought over Nyandwara's attention and affection. She was powerful and had a profound influence over our parents, so it was always safe to be on her side. You can therefore imagine my apprehension when I went to fetch water in Oroba and broke Nyandwara's pot. It was a small pot. I slipped and fell on Kabar's wet black cotton soil and Nyandwara's's precious pot broke into many shattered pieces.

I was only eight then. I cried as the other children laughed at me, afraid of Nyandwara's wrath and loss of favour. But she was kind about it and made little fuss over the incident. I observed a soft nature of Nyandwara I had not seen before, one that she hid from the public. She was not vindictive. Not like Donata.

Pots are like love; once broken they cannot be put back together again. Pots are like trust; once broken they cannot be repaired.

The cracked pieces rebelliously defy the moulder's hands as they go their separate ways. That was what happened when Donata broke her pot on my back. I escaped with scathing wounds, with painful scars that turned my life around, brought such drastic changes to my life and almost cost me my dear life.

Donata appeared in the form of an apparition of the *Nyawawa* spirits cast loose from the belly of Lake Victoria, vengeful spirits of angry water gods out to wreak havoc in people's lives. Gods that were offended by the local community because it had failed to give decent burials to the dead, especially to corpses whose bones lay scattered and abandoned in the murky waters. Their spirits raged like storms and overturned ships and boats with travellers and fishermen aboard. They left a trail of deaths, illnesses and misery along their path as they headed to the Nandi hills. They howled and growled and sang unintelligible songs that sounded sad and scary. Children often hid in fear under their beds as adults beat empty tins to scare them away.

I lost whatever trust and respect I had for the ICC and its investigators. I lost respect for the court. I wondered what kind of justice this court of last resort could give if the people behind it committed such grave injustice through their carelessness and refused to take responsibility for their actions.

I went on the run, hoping to avoid death, often missing death by a whisker. I would arrive at a place to hide, only to find that death had just left moments before I got there. At times, I got a warning that death was very close, on its way to my hiding place, moments before I arrived.

I knew death was coming for me; I felt it rather close, I could see it, I could hear it. I could feel it in the air. It would be through a hail of bullets or one well targeted shot at my chest. I was afraid, terribly afraid and all because of Donata.

Donata introduced herself to me as an investigator from the ICC. She was from Ocampo's vineyard – the great lion prosecutor who had instilled unforgettable fear and terror in the hearts of Kenyans after the 2007/08 PEV.

When Donata called, I was quite busy. I had just held a well-attended young professional media women's luncheon at my home, which also served as my office, in Woodley, off Ngong Road, Nairobi. It also housed the Media Liaison and Advocacy Centre for journalists.

We had great plans. I would mentor the young women to be professionals, to avoid corruption and to establish themselves as respectable journalists. We were excited, hopeful and ready for the high seas. But that was not to be.

The Media Liaison and Advocacy Resource Centre was a hub for journalists. Members came in, read newspapers and journals, watched television, made coffee as they did their research. I had set up six working stations with six new computers and one extra laptop, from my modest life savings of about Kshs1.2 million. We had a huge bed and comfortable armchairs where sleepy and tired journalists could fall into a heap and sleep out their exhaustion after chasing a story. It was indeed a journalists' world.

The centre had printers, a well-stocked library with thousands of literature and journalism books, collections of old and current newspapers and magazines. As a student of literature and later journalism, I had invested rather heavily in books. We were set for a promising future. The four most devoted journalists in my group - Sheila, Mary, Caro and Lillian - were always by my side, full of hope, a real epitome of enthusiasm. I had registered my organisation at Sheria House, where it had taken three months of waiting but finally, the certificate had come out. We danced in celebration, now sure that nothing would disrupt our goals.

Donata's call disrupted my whole programme. It threw everything into disarray and left the young journalists without direction because I had to go underground suddenly. I had conducted job interviews and got a young lady journalist, Susan, to run the centre. The organisation's website was ready. All these became history, on the spur of a moment, in the twinkle of an eye.

I missed friends' funerals and birthdays and other important work-related events and had no time to explain what had happened. Others would judge, I knew. But they did not know what I had gone through in those few months. They did not know why my phone was off when they needed me most and how frequently I had to renew my number at the Safaricom centres and buy new phones. My priority was to save my life.

This Donata business rekindled an experience I had long forgotten, opened an old wound that lay buried somewhere in my past. After school, we would often sneak into the lake to swim. But this was brought to a stop after a traumatic experience – a Hague-like experience.

I was about ten and in class five. My classmates and I planned to go and swim in the snake, crocodile and hippo-infested waters of Lake Victoria. We quickly threw off our uniforms and jumped into the water. One of my friends, Katumba, was unfortunate. She stepped on a crocodile, disguised as a rock and the last we heard of her was her screams as the crocodile dived away with her body deep into the blood coloured water.

We all ran home in fear, stark naked. We had forgotten to carry our uniforms on the spur of the moment. I never went back to the lake again until decades later as an adult.

Yet it was not only the organisation I lost. My encounter with Donata forced me to abandon my dog, Happy, and my cat, Jolawi. I hoped and prayed that Happy and Jolawi would not die from a broken heart.

"Donata, Donata, why did you damage my life? Where did you come from - daughter of The Hague? Who sent you?" These questions rang in my mind often.

If only she was a cat or a dog, things would not have turned out so bad. But she was neither a cat nor a dog. I held a grudge against Donata for what she had done to me. I wished her ill.

Nyandwara was my Baba's mother. She had a special place for me in her heart. She had named me "Omwa", after her daughter who had died. She had seven sons and Omwa Nyakisia was the first daughter she had after 16 years of trying for a girl. Everyone fondly called her "Nyaki", a corrupted version of "Nyako", which means girl. But at the age of three, Nyaki just stretched out one evening after supper and died shortly afterwards. Just like that. The only daughter in a family of seven boys, over-loved, petted, spoilt like a cat. Nyaki's death broke Nyandwara's heart.

When I was born many years later and my Baba and my Mama named me "Nyaki", Nyandwara was relieved. It was as if Nyaki, Nyandwara's daughter, had been reincarnated. I was given lots of love by my uncles who were at the same time my "brothers". They called me "my sister" and not "my niece" as they did with my siblings. My aunt and her female cousin were my "sisters" while at the same time my "mothers". This meant I was, according to tradition, an aunt to my siblings and to all my cousins. My nieces and nephews called me both "aunt" and "grandmother".

Nyandwara was wise. She would have solved this Donata puzzle in minutes. She would have found a quick solution to Donata's eerie visitation. But she was no more. How I missed her! How I missed her sincere grandmotherly, philosophical and practical ways of handling life's challenges. I missed my deceased maternal grandparents, Lorna Ayieko and Zablon Misala too. A home without grandparents is like a deserted homestead. It remains empty, pillars of wisdom shamefully buried with its owners in the underworld.

For a long time, I could not forgive Donata. I agonised over why she turned against me. I wondered whether the people I sent to her to let her know I was in trouble and wanted to meet her had given her the right message.

Life's experiences had proved that not all messengers delivered the message as required. Others had turned traitors and distorted the message, taking advantage of the situation to satiate their greed and other selfish interests.

A man could send his best friend to pay dowry for his wife only to hear that the friend had eloped with his bride. Could this have happened in my case? I did not know. I would never know, as all my attempts, requests to meet Donata had been met with a stoic silence. And then the painful words, "she has said she does not want to meet you. You have already been interfered with." I was on my own. I could be wrong but from the little information I gathered, Donata was upset because one of my lawyers had directly contacted her boss to find out why she wanted to meet me.

My lawyer had also reported to Donata's boss that strange fellows were following me. It seems that Donata's boss had caused a fuss over Donata's careless approach in handling my matter. I was now exposed and my life was in danger. An angry Donata then became vindictive and sent an e-mail to my lawyer, saying she was no longer interested in meeting me. But the damage was already done. True or not, I shall never know. At least that is what I gathered from my intelligence network.

CHAPTER FOUR

Life on Hold

I REPORTED TO AND RECORDED A STATEMENT at the Criminal Investigation Department (CID) headquarters in Kilimani, Nairobi, accompanied by the Kenya National Commission on Human Rights (KNCHR) officials. My life was in danger. The CID officer who recorded my statement was so terrified that he refused to append his name to my statement, claiming he did not want to be associated with The Hague.

"My children are still young and I want to retire in peace. I do not want to be summoned to The Hague to explain your statement," he told us.

The police officer was seven-foot tall, dark and sprightly. He tried to be as brave as possible but his whole body shook, his fingers trembled. He paused in between to wipe off the involuntary sweat from the palm of his moist hands with his faded blue tie. At times, he walked out of the room to take a quick breath of fresh air, then came back in to continue. He glanced over his shoulder now and then as if The Hague's eyes watched his every step, as if someone could snatch him from his seat in a whisker and puff the light out of him. Three Human Rights officers who had accompanied me to the police station seemed familiar with handling dangerous cases. They waited patiently until the interview was over then handed me safely back to my protection officers at my Safe House.

Strange people followed me everywhere, hang around my flat since the day Donata called me.

My phone was tapped then later blocked. I could not make or receive any calls. All the contacts in my phone and all messages and history were deleted. My e-mails were hacked and I was getting strange e-mails sent from myself to myself.

My mind flashed back to the pre-election violence period. Who could have anticipated such unprecedented violence after results were announced? We set off as a battalion of coastal region reporters hot on the heels of politicians. Campaigns were the heart of journalism reporting in Kenya. Our mornings started at 3 am. We covered PEV in Coast Province where I was a Bureau Chief with a local newspaper. Our beat was various politicians, especially the presidential candidates Mwai Kibaki, Raila Odinga and Kalonzo Musyoka through their political campaigns.

We trailed first lady, Lucy Kibaki, in Lamu as she campaigned for her husband as the most intelligent man in the country, with first-class honours in Economics from the prestigious Makerere University in Uganda. We plagued the famous, controversial "activist" in Coast as she campaigned for her President, Mwai Kibaki and taunted her with personal questions, which she ignored. What she did not fail to reiterate was her love for Kibaki and his outstanding credentials.

The politicians were oratory masters and mistresses. Their honey-tongued words drew crowds to their nest as we followed PNU with their *"Kibaki Tena"* campaigns. Politicians made dangerous remarks and threatened to clear all *madoadoa* (spots) from their midst. Voters drew in the words like their breath of life.

When Donata called, she asked to meet me and discuss some issues regarding Post Election Violence and the role of certain politicians in the ensuing chaos. She told me the International Criminal Court had gathered and thoroughly scrutinised media reports from local media sources on the goings on in Kenya prior to and after elections and wished to have a chat with me regarding some articles. The connection was not very clear and we called each other back and forth until she finally called from an audible line.

I asked Donata who had given her my contacts but she did not disclose her source. She merely cited, 'media sources.'

In my journalism career that spanned over ten years, it was never an option to disclose one's sources. Many journalists had gone to jail over failure to disclose a source. It was a matter of honour, a matter of media ethics.

To disclose a source, especially a whistle blower, was betrayal of the highest order. Not only would you lose the trust that had been bestowed upon you, but colleagues would also despise you.

You could also lose your sources and no one would ever give you a story to publish again. Although she declined to reveal her source, Donata sounded friendly and I thought I liked her. She inquired if I could pay her a visit to their offices in Kilimani Law Courts. I had guests so I could not leave.

"It's out of my way and I am busy now," I told her. "Where are you? I can come right where you are," she said.

"Ok, come to Ngong Road, Nakumatt Prestige, Swahili Plate in about an hour!" I told her.

"Alright, I am on my way."

Swahili Plate – a 10-minute walk from my house was my favourite place for authentic, mouth-watering coastal *Pilau* and *Biriani* dishes. Being a regular customer, the staff there knew me well. I felt safe meeting the stranger, Donata, there.

When Donata's call first came through, my sister Susana*, who had listened to the conversation keenly, was aghast. She had just come back home after her two-year study in the Netherlands. She had arrived in Nairobi a day earlier and had come to see me. Susana was accompanied by our niece Viola* (12) and Viola's dog, Simba, which she had received as a birthday gift.

"You must be shrewd," Susana advised. It was obvious she had eavesdropped on our conversation. She is six years older than I and hers was always the voice of reason. "How can you even tell the call is from The Hague? You may go there and get shot. Be wise, ask the lady to give you her credentials on e-mail as you consult further," she warned.

My sister Susana's logic stopped me dead on my tracks. I had not looked at the whole issue holistically. What if this was not Donata but a trickster? Was I safe? Was it wise to meet her at a public place?

"The Hague is an international court. They cannot just call you like that. It's probably someone playing a prank – probably one of your friends or colleagues pretending to be a white woman. They are very systematic and professional. Anyway, to get a second opinion, just call Seraphine* and hear what she must say," Susana advised.

Seraphine is our sister, a general practice lawyer who is always give relatives free legal advice. We often take advantage of her whenever we need legal advice. But Seraphine has a heart of gold and she never complains. She goes out of her way whenever we approach her as a family and always ensures justice is done.

She is my late Baba, reincarnated. Seraphine immediately dismissed the matter. "Ignore the call for now," she said. "If she is really from The Hague and really needs to see you, she will definitely look for you again. For now, you had better switch off the phone so that whoever she is, she may not reach you."

"Are you sure you really want to be a witness? Are you sure

you know what you are getting into? Being a witness is a full-time job, you know!"

As I consulted Seraphine over the phone, Susana had already called my Mama and reported what had transpired. As soon as I finished with Seraphine, my Mama called.

"My daughter, what is this I am hearing? I understand you have evidence against The Hague suspects? And you are supposed to be a witness? Be very careful. You know these people are very powerful and the government is on their side. Think very carefully over the matter, but if I were you, I would keep a very safe distance," my Mama, wise in her 80s, advised.

Why was everybody so cautious, so negative about this meeting? I wondered.

Deep in my heart, I really wanted to meet Donata and hear what she had to say. I hated unfinished business and I wanted this whole Donata stuff over and done with.

I like to keep my word. I really felt bad that Donata probably waited at the Swahili Plate as agreed. To ensure I did not leave immediately, Susana who had been in a hurry to leave before Donata's call, now seemed to take her sweet time, offering to clear the dishes after lunch.

No sooner had I talked to my Mama than my younger brother Steve, * a banker, called.

"I hear Ocampo himself has called you and asked you to co-operate with the ICC court, please switch off your phone immediately and do not respond to any strange numbers. Keep off trouble," he advised.

News travels fast, especially within a large family. And usually by the time word goes around and comes back, it is not likely to be in the original form in which it was told, meant or intended. My Mama had raised 13 children, including those of relatives and all of us were healthy and alive, thanks to God's great mercy. My Baba had died in a tragic road accident 14 years ago. He was a banker and my brother Steve took after him.

He had left all his children well educated and well established. We were a large family indeed but monogamous.

On the surface, I pretended to take advice from my family but told myself that as soon as my sister, niece and Simba – the friendly dog – left, I could slip into the Swahili Plate and meet Donata for all it was worth. But as fate would have it, I never got to meet Donata.

As my niece Viola opened the door, Simba seemed excited that they were leaving. He jumped on me, knocking down my phone. The phone fell into pieces. He took the battery, licked it playfully and dashed with it to the grass outside.

He left the battery at the neighbour's doorstep, ran back to me and jumped on me with his wet dirty paws, making me smell doggy. I bid my sister and niece goodbye and went into the bathroom for a shower. I picked the battery, cleaned it, put it back on the phone, and it worked.

At 12.45 pm, I left my home/office and walked on the sidewalk to Nakumatt Prestige to meet Donata the meeting place. At an intersection of Mugo Kibiru Road, I passed two special branch security officers standing. They stared at me with expressionless faces. My mind was deep in thought so I walked on without giving it a thought.

A few minutes later, I noticed that the two men I had just passed were walking hurriedly behind me. I did not think anything of it and I continued walking and soon arrived at the mall where I entered the supermarket. The men were now trailing me on different aisles. I escaped from the supermarket and entered an adjacent cafe and sat down. They also entered the cyber cafe and sat down. I ordered for a glass of fresh passion juice. They also ordered for a glass of fresh passion juice. I left them sitting down and rushed into a restaurant on the ground floor. I sat on an empty seat at the restaurant, catching my breath. The two security officers soon found me and sat about two tables away from me.

I was terribly afraid. I confirmed they were the dreaded State Security agents, probably from a unit of the Special Branch because of their dressing. They were both dressed in ill-fitting, over washed navy-blue suits, bright blue shirts, and navy blue ties. Their suit jackets had a badge with lapels on the left breast pocket with a coat of arms and a Kenyan flag; the trademark of the Special Branch. Their clean-shaven heads did not help. I had become truly alarmed at this point.

From the nature of my work, I had seen State Security agents when I covered presidential or state functions or election campaigns of senior government ministers so I had no doubt in my mind who these people were. I had seen these people running after the President's car at every presidential function. They also jumped ahead of the President's car at every function, pushing anybody on their way. Sometimes they pushed journalists who covered presidential functions and at times even broke their cameras.

I knew Donata was upstairs, waiting for me. She had described herself and asked me to look out for an elderly white woman carrying a pink handbag. I had also described myself to her as a slim, tall, dark lady with short hair. The sound of imaginary gunshots triggered by fear rang in my brain.

I became so terrified that I exited the mall and never got to meet Donata on the next floor. I was not sure whether Donata was alone or whether these people were part of her plan to have me kidnapped. The mall was not crowded as it would be around that time and it was obvious that the Special Branch agents were not trying to hide the fact that they were following me. I called my taxi driver, Ndung'u Nderitu, on my cell phone and told him to pick me up at the entrance in about three minutes. He was my most trusted driver who dropped and picked me from work when I was a sub-editing consultant at a Features Service in Nairobi. My task was how to escape from both Donata and these agents. My heart was pumping like a posho mill engine. I pretended not to be in a hurry to leave but after about two and a half minutes, I abruptly got up and left. I did not look back to see if I was being followed.

At the entrance of the Nakumatt supermarket, Nderitu was just pulling into the pick-up area. I jumped into the back of the taxi and he pulled out and into Ngong Road. I told him there were strange men following me and asked him to lose them if he saw them trailing us. He told me that he saw them through the rear view standing by the entrance but they did not try to follow us.

The taxi driver made several turns just to make sure nobody was following us. We dodged the heavy traffic, now piling up on Ngong Road from the City Mortuary, Nairobi Baptist Church, Daystar University, China Centre, and Yaya Centre junction, towards Adams Arcade. He drove me round and round past Our Lady of Guadalupe Church, Uchumi supermarket, and Moi Nairobi Girls High School. We drove around Nairobi for several hours before returning home.

By then, I was deeply worried. Who were these people following me and why, immediately after Donata's call? Was it a mere coincidence? Were they the ones who had called? Did Donata really exist? Was I dreaming? What was all this? It felt like a bad dream, like the day my Baba and my Mama were involved in a road accident. I could not believe that my dear loving Baba had died on the spot and my Mama and sister were in a coma with broken limbs. It still hurts decades later that such a terrible dream had turned out to be true. Death was such a bad dream, yet such a painful reality. What irony!

I got back in my house at about 7.00pm. I drew the curtains but decided not to switch on the lights. I mixed some hot water from the flask on my study table with two tea spoons of sugar and two tea spoons of coffee to make it strong. I was exhausted but sleep was the last thing on my mind.

I called Safari to find out if he knew of any ICC investigation of journalists going on in the country but he did not pick up his phone.

I breathed deeply, and then decided to ignore the whole situation. "This can't be. I'm probably dreaming," I told myself. "None of this is happening, it happens only in movies and newspapers. Calm down. Get real," I kept telling myself. I pinched myself painfully on my wrist to ensure that it was I, Nyaki, going through this strange experience.

I went to bed early without switching on the lights. I pushed the huge study table against the door – just in case, you never know. I hoped that by the time I woke up in the morning, all would be well and the dream would be over. I tossed over and over in bed the whole night like a *mahamri* in hot oil. It was a cold May and the usually cold June weather in Nairobi had set in earlier than expected. But I sweated profusely and kicked off the warm pink duvet. I did not sleep that night. And all was not well.

I had switched off my phone before going to bed the previous night. After a serious pep talk with myself, I decided to switch on my phone and take the bull by its horns. I checked the clock on the wall, it was 5.00am. Two short text messages beeped on my phone. One was from Donata and it said, "We are still waiting at the Swahili Plate." She must have sent it at about 3.00pm the day before. The second one was from Safari. "I called you back but your phone was off, please get in touch."

I waited up to 8.00am then called Safari.

"I got a strange call from a woman claiming to be an ICC investigator and I was terrified. That is why I had switched off my phone," I explained. That was when Safari reminded me of a story way back in 2007, in which I had confessed to a confrontation I had with one of The Hague suspects whose agent wanted to corrupt me with Kshs2 million. It was now 2012 and my mind was foggy over this issue that had happened five years back.

"It is to do with Mr Ruto. Do you remember after you had a situation with him and after this story was published you received threats from strange persons? That is what The Hague wants to discuss with you," Safari explained.

Coast was not a hotspot for Post-Election Violence like Naivasha, Kisumu, Nakuru and Eldoret. There were spontaneous riots in Mombasa regarding the elections results, but not any deaths of non-Coastal communities that I knew of. There were forceful evictions of Kenyans who allegedly belonged to the PNU party or who, because of being Kikuyu or Kamba were believed to have voted for Kibaki. Angry mobs flushed them out of their homes and shops but after intervention by police and sober neighbours, everyone was allowed back to their homes. One of those threatened by a mob was a journalist in my office, whom I helped sneak out of the Coast after his house was attacked.

"It is true that the call is from ICC. In fact, I am the one who gave them your contacts. You remember the story I interviewed you over called, "Dirty Hands"? I mean the investigative story on corruption in the media? You remember how strangers threatened you after the story was published in Expression Today? Anyway, don't worry. You are not the only one ICC is investigating. They have already talked to other journalists and I know some who have agreed to be witnesses, but under pseudonyms," Safari explained. His tirade did not console me. I did not understand why he had given my name to the ICC as a potential witness.

"Well Safari, why didn't you alert me or tell me to expect

their call? You should have at least called and asked me if I was willing to talk to them?" I chided him.

Safari was unapologetic. I felt as if he diminished or did not understand what impact his actions could have in my life "Well, there is no need for you to fuss. They just want to have a general chat with you," he replied.

"Anyway, I am not happy about the ambush but since it's already done, I will meet them. I already "bounced" their meeting. Should they get in touch with you, ask them to feel free to call me," I said.

"I do not have Donata's number so should she be in touch again, please ask her to call me," I told Safari.

"Okay," Safari said.

I called my Mama and told her I was going to meet Donata and find out what exactly she had in mind.

"I have prayed about it, my Mama, and I think it is the right thing to do," I told her.

"The decision is really yours, my daughter. It is a personal choice. If your conscience is clear, all you really need to do is to speak the truth, just like your late Baba and your grandmother would have done. Remember though, whatever decision you make, you have my support. I will stand by you, I will pray for you," my Mama replied.

I also got hold of one of my editors, Dick*, on Facebook and we talked online. His advice was a lot like my mother's.

"If your conscience is clear about this, Nyaki, go ahead and meet this ICC investigator. All you need to do is tell them the truth. What you must realise is that this is a very serious situation that's going to change your life forever. If I were you, I'd do it. You have my support!" he said.

After talking to my Mama and my editor, I felt relieved. As I confidently moved to the window to draw open the curtains, I saw the same two security agents walking past my window.

A sharp fear pricked my heart. I stopped dead on my tracks, as if paralysed. I was not dreaming. It was true. I was being observed. What could I do? I peeped through the curtains. The security agents went around the field twice and then they sat at the corner where the young estate boys smoked their cigarette and bhang every evening. They stared at my house.

I felt besieged and confused. Never had I felt death so close. I knew my life would never be the same again.

I was supposed to have a session with some of the young female journalists at 10.00am. I called them and cancelled the session. I stayed indoors and continued with my work. Not long before Donata's call, I had come from Saidia children's home in Gilgil to follow up a story on a young boy, Ryan Brownstead, who had been allegedly abused by her aunt.

The story and the pictures were depressing and although we journalists are usually advised not to get emotionally involved in the story, we are human too and often get depressed by some incidents.

A considerable number of children in the home had been thrown out in the forest or left by the roadside after birth, then rescued by police.

Meanwhile, I waited patiently for Donata to call again.

I switched on my laptop and googled the story, 'Dirty Hands'. It was quite a while back since I did the interview. The story had been published in 2010, but the incidents surrounding the story had been in 2007 or thereabout.

As I read the article, I realized why the ICC was interested in me. I had rejected an ICC suspect's agent's offer of millions and land in Eldoret. I suspected the ICC wanted to follow up on the suspect's corruption pattern and his ability to corrupt witnesses.

"My employer pays me more money than I need," I had told his aide back then, and laughed contemptuously at his offer. Whenever I came across such temptations during my work, I would guard myself with my late Baba's words of wisdom.

"My daughter, there is nothing as sweet and fulfilling in this world as the money you have worked for, as the money you have earned from the sweat of your brows." That was my mantra. The mantra I repeated to politicians' corrupt agents as I turned down their dirty money. The mantra I dared repeat to anyone who was cheeky enough to offer me a bribe to hush their story, to cover up corruption. That is why it was so easy for me to return the Kshs50,000 I found on my desk from a water company in Mombasa. They wanted me to hush their story on corruption.

That is why I had found it so easy to return the Kshs2500 brought to my office by an agent of IAAF athletics official during the World Championships during my stint in Mombasa.

I seemed to have made many enemies both within and without. Kenya was a corrupt society through and through and people did not like it if you did not eat with them or became a stumbling block to their short-cuts. My grandmother Nyandwara had been a proud one too. She would have done the same and warned everyone in the village to stop thinking she was cheap enough to take a bribe.

She did not like free gifts and would always show off her granary – full of her hard-earned grains – maize, beans and green grams.

Her chicken proudly pecked the soil all over the compound and never came into the house during meals to peck at guests' feet as often happened in some homes. It was as if they had learnt from their owner the art of survival, the need to hunt for one's own food. At no time would one visit my grandmother Nyandwara's home and find her granary empty. If we had no salt, we would do without it. "Missing salt in your meal for a few days will not kill you!" she would say.

If there is one major character I can thank Nyandwara for, is that she taught me to be independent.

My frustrations in Coast Province got deeper, especially coming from the head office, and I quietly planned my exit from the job. Now, as I sat in my house in Woodley, I tried to analyse the "dirty hands" story.

I seemed to have made many enemies. I knew that despite the facts of the story being true, it was against media ethics to stand as a witness in a court and quote a source.

I had just launched my organisation, "Media Liaison and Advocacy Consultants which focused on Media Ethics and Responsible Journalism. Its mantra was, "Keeping the fire of professionalism alive."

The Mombasa experience motivated me to start this dream professional mentorship organisation for young female journalists. As a professional, one need not feel insecure.

I would meet Donata, but I would explain to her that it would be against media ethics to be a witness. Still, I would give her any useful information she needed.

Donata called a week later on a Sunday evening and I knew then that matters were elephant. She was serious. In her friendly, soft voice, she kindly queried why I had stood her up.

I explained to her how the dog Simba had messed up my phone, and although she sounded shocked at my naïve excuse, we simply laughed it off. I was growing fond of Donata and I wanted to co-operate with her. I apologised for having kept her waiting and she quickly brushed it off – rather graciously. I wanted to find a way of telling her what had transpired but I was not sure of who was listening to our conversation. I did not trust Donata yet.

She said she had enjoyed one of the Swahili dishes and learnt about the new eating place. She had already gone back to The Hague and informed me of her busy schedule. She promised she would be back the following Sunday.

"If I cannot make it, I will send two of my colleagues in Nairobi to meet you," she said.

"They are welcome, although I would have preferred to meet you," I said.

I knew Donata genuinely had a busy schedule. That week, Ocampo - outgoing chief prosecutor at The Hague - was to visit Kenya and introduce the new prosecutor, Fatou Bensouda to the Kenyan Government.

But some members of Parliament had threatened to disrupt the visit and for some reason (I guess related to the threat), the visit had been postponed. Ocampo had instead thanked Kenyans in a live television address for the warm reception and support he had received from ordinary Kenyan people and for the opportunity they had given him to serve them. He said he had a special place for Kenyans in his heart.

The turn of events was not surprising. Some Kenyan politicians threatened to strip naked if some of the ICC suspects were indicted.

The Government was on an urgent shuttle diplomacy around the world, particularly the Africa Union and the UN Security Council. She sought deferral for these cases from The Hague. The Government tried to bring the trials "back home". Kenyan Parliament voted several times against a local tribunal using the now infamous quote, "Don't be vague, go to The Hague."

Government wanted to have her cake and eat it. At the initial stages of the pre-trial, the same Government had offered to pay legal fees for the suspects and to get them some of the best lawyers in the world. The same Government had allegedly refused to cooperate with the ICC prosecutors to gather evidence against the indictees, although Kenya is a signatory to the Rome Statute which created the ICC.

There was no sympathy, not a single word for the victims and no indication whether the government felt anything for them.

The hypocrisy, the dishonesty of politicians remained a talent no one could take away from them. I wondered how chaotic it would be in our courts of law if all relatives and friends stripped naked every day at each hearing.

The trial conference for the four Kenyan ICC suspects was to start soon after Donata's call. I called my friend Wolf in Belgium and informed him of what was going on. I tried to email him a copy of the story "dirty hands" but he told me his mail was blocked. Wolf advised me to get in touch with the Committee to Protect Journalists for advice.

The same uniformed men followed me when I went to the kiosk to ask Mama Mboga if I could use her phone. They made no attempt to hide and, at one point, I felt they wanted me to know they watched me. As the two security agents walked behind me, I started sweating profusely. I thought I would get a gun shot on my back. One image after another of prominent Kenyans who had disappeared only to be found dead came to my mind. These deaths had been linked to state agents but no evidence had been found. I saw a picture of the late Nyandarua MP, J.M. Kariuki, whose body had been found in the thickets of Ngong Forest. Then I saw another horrid picture of the charred remains of the late former Minister for Foreign Affairs, Robert Ouko, the brilliant diplomat whose remains had been traced to the foot of Got Alila Hills in Koru, Nyanza. His body, found by a herdsman called Shikuku, had been burnt beyond recognition in what appeared to be some chemical.

A government pathologist's report had implied that the late Minister had shot himself and then burnt his own body by douching it in acid! And then where was Shikuku; how come he could not be traced after that? Painful images of Oscar Kingara killed on State House Road tore my heart. I was not prominent. I was just a mere journalist seeking the truth with a mighty sword – the pen. But the fact that the ICC had approached me regarding an ICC indictee put me in such a precarious situation that I saw images of myself shot dead, hidden in some thicket in Ngong Hills. I was perceived to have powerful information that could put suspects behind bars for years.

I disappeared into the market at the Kibera junction and bought credit cards at the Kengen Petrol Station. I was afraid to go back to my house. I took my time "window shopping" inside the market until it got dark. That night, I moved around the house without the lights on again.

It was becoming my new way of life. I felt intimidated. I followed a different path back to my house, loaded my modem in one of the computers at my work station and informed CPJ by Skype that I was still being followed. I panicked. I tried to seek a visa from the Belgian Embassy where my man-friend Wolf lived. After calling Wolf through a friend's number, he had invited me to go over and stay at his place until things cooled down. But the embassy needed corroboration from the ICC that they had indeed approached me. So, they e-mailed the ICC and asked me to hold on. An e-mail response from the ICC denying that they knew me or had even tried to get in touch with me came to the Embassy. Mr Dan Desmadryl, the consular, sent me a curt e-mail denying me a visa and asked me to explain that I was not lying!

This convinced me more than ever at that time that Donata was a fake and did not actually exist.

My family and I were therefore very concerned that I was now in the middle of a very dangerous internal and international criminal and political affair affecting two of the most powerful politicians in the country. I was very fearful for my life and I did not know what to do. I was caught between the devil and the deep blue sea.

Karoli*, the CPJ contact person for Eastern Africa, advised me to leave my house immediately and move in with a friend, not a relative or any family member. Meanwhile, Karoli also communicated with Wolf to see how he could assist me to leave the country. He further consulted several Human Rights organisations to access Safe Houses. I called my taxi man, Nderitu, in the morning, picked my bag and left the house. I was on the run. I passed by Steve's office, dumped my laptop and phone with him and begged him to throw them in the nearest dust bin.

"It's easy to locate anyone using the laptop and phone. It would be safe for me if you threw them away as I make my escape," I told him.

Nderitu then dropped me somewhere along River Road, in Nairobi's downtown where I made my next move.

Thus, began my life as a fugitive in my own country. I did not know where to go. My genuine friends had always been within the family – apart from one or two people. I had hoped to move in with my friend Joan but when I passed by her office, she told me the situation was too dangerous and she did not want to be involved. "I am a public figure, you know, and everyone knows I am your closest friend. It is my house they will come to look for you first." She gave me Kshs1000 and wished me well.

She was philosophical and I understood her. It was not her. It was the fear of The Hague. The fear of The Hague was real. According to the Hansard, some members of Parliament confessed to sleepless nights because they had dreams that they were in Ocampo's list, which he was about to release before the pre-trials. One Member of Parliament had told the speaker that she had skipped Parliament several times due to lack of sleep over Hague matters. She claimed she had dreamt she was in Ocampo's list of suspects and that her dreams often turned out to be true! The people whose help I sought did not believe my story. This hurt me deeply. It was as if I was the only sane one and everyone around me was mad. Or they were all sane and I was mad.

I had my house rent and an additional Kshs2000 my brother had given me. I walked quickly down River Road and found a bus ready for Mombasa. Without a second thought, I dived and almost knocked down the conductor at the door. "Ala, Ma! Are you running away from your husband's beatings?" He probed. I did not respond. I quickly paid Kshs900 for the ticket. It was 1.00 pm and the rain fell mercilessly outside. The bus left for Mombasa at 8.00 pm. My new life had begun.

The ticket conductor did not ask for my name and in a way, this gave me a temporary sense of security. He just gave me a ticket in exchange for the money. He seemed to enjoy the Taarab music now playing loudly in his tape. The sweet smell of the rain meeting the earth made me feel alive.

Cold breeze came in through the window and I wrapped my thick warm brown fur coat around me. It was a gift from my sister Joan when I first travelled to Amsterdam for an international assignment. I had then accompanied Mr Ababu Namwamba (later to be Budalangi Member of Parliament) to receive the "Save the Children Debt" award. Some passengers seemed to enjoy the lyrics too and sang along.

As we moved further away from Nairobi, the language in the bus changed into fluent lyrical Kiswahili, with a deep Coastal accent. The snacks travellers ate in the bus –coconuts, pilau, *mahamri* made with *iliki* – were Swahili delicacies.

Women with henna on their nails and toes and different Piko designs on their arms all displayed Swahili culture. Most female passengers wore black *Buibui* and *Hijabs*, the Swahili gown of honour.

I made a mental note to buy one as soon as I alighted in Mwembe Tayari to disguise myself. At Mtito Andei, the passenger next to me alighted and someone else came to sit next to me. He offered me a soda but I declined, shaking my head vigorously. My Mama had advised me from childhood never to accept food from strangers. Media reports were rampant with passengers who had accepted drinks and snacks from fellow passengers only to find themselves drugged – they woke up stark naked, in a strange town, without luggage and their money. They could not even recall their names or where they were travelling to. The passenger seemed offended that I had rejected his drink, "Mama, I have no ill motives. Why do you refuse my drink? Do you suspect I want to drug you?" he asked.

I did not respond or look at him. Instead, I looked straight ahead and pulled my mouth into a long no nonsense pout. A conversation with a stranger seemed like an unnecessary hazard in times like these. I was not going to draw attention to myself. I was on the run and drama was the last thing I wanted. The man finally kept quiet and closed his eyes. He alighted at the next stop and disappeared into the cold rainy dark night.

CHAPTER FIVE

Unfinished Business

I stayed in Mombasa for only ten days. I had worked at the Coast and knew my way around. When I left Nairobi, I did not know exactly where in Mombasa I would end up, but along the way I weighed options. My first thought was to seek refuge at my former landlord, Mr Bashraheel's home in Ganjoni. Bashraheel and his wife were kind to me throughout my stay in Coast and treated me like family.

When I first reported to Mombasa as Bureau Chief, I encountered the stark reality of tribalism in Kenyan. Threats were a rife part of my media work, especially at my level. I received threatening calls daily on my phone asking me to vacate Coast Province. The callers said there was no room for aliens *(watu wa Bara)*. I was distressed. The colleagues I asked to help me look for a house frankly informed me that many landlords had said they would not allow a Luo tenant in their premises since Luos in Coast Province had a reputation of not paying rent!

"Besides, Luos are very proud. When you ask them to pay rent, they will look at their watches and tell you to come back after one month as they are very busy in a meeting. They also play loud music when they are bereaved and disrupt people's sleep in the residence. But the worst thing about Luos is that married couples are always engaged in physical brawls at home. They break doors and windows and leave the house in tatters!"

Surely, I am Kenyan and could work and live in any part of the country, if I was qualified. I silently soldiered on and bore the heavy brunt of being discriminated against because of my tribe.

The threats grew worse when I exposed a scandal involving buying of the Kenya National Exams (KNEC) Form Four papers. After a tip from a member of the public, I bought the Mathematics and Kiswahili papers through a source, a day before the final paper. When I took the papers to the police station, the police asked me to mind my own business if I knew what was good for me. When I called the exam head office in Nairobi, the KNEC secretary told me I was dreaming and no one cheated in exams. I was fortunate the editors had faith in my story. They published the expose on the front page and sent the country reeling in anger.

The Exam Council came out fighting against the story. They denied and dismissed the obvious. More threats came on my phone, as late as midnight, warning me that they would kill me if I pursued the story. I lost faith in the Kenya Police and in the national examinations. Just like I had lost faith in the ICC, Donata, and everything to do with international justice. Things were not what they seemed. People were not really what they were or appeared to be. I was learning the hard way. That truth did not necessarily give you peace or justice. It did not earn one friends, but more enemies.

Bashraheel and my Baba had both worked at the Kenya Commercial Bank (KCB), at different times. He was a branch manager in Nairobi and Mombasa while my Baba was a Credit Controller in Kisumu. After I rented his premises for almost one-and-a-half years, he felt sad when I informed him that I was transferred back to the head office in Nairobi and would no longer be his tenant.

"You have been a good tenant. Whenever you come back to Mombasa, our home is always open for you. You do not need to pay rent at a Five Star Hotel." That was a place to seek refuge.

You can imagine my disappointment when I alighted at Mwembe Tayari at 5.00am and took a *tuktuk* to Ganjoni, hung outside the door until 7.00am, rang the doorbell several times and got no response!

A hostile well-built woman in a foul mood and a hurriedly tied *leso* asked me rather rudely what I wanted.

"The landlord no longer lives here. He sold this building and moved with his family to Kisumu," she said.

I crossed over the street, just a two-minute walk from the house to the Oceanic Sand hotel. It was right opposite my old house below the landlord's flat. I had never imagined that I would stay there. But times had changed. Although I wanted to check in under the name 'Saida,' to keep anyone who may have followed me off track, a young Muslim woman living alone in a guest house would easily have aroused suspicion.

"Name?" the lady receptionist asked. "Tumi," I replied. She did not ask for my identity card and I breathed a sigh of relief. I paid Kshs1100 bed only and climbed upstairs to my room on the third floor.

I had some fond memories of Coast where I had worked for close to two years between 2007 and 2008 as Bureau Chief before getting transferred back to Nairobi. The elephant dance at Shimba Hills in Kwale had been fascinating. It was a show of power and might. Yet anyone having watched the elephants of Mt Elgon – broken down, wailing and burying their dead could not imagine how life's tragedies could break down even the strongest of us all. Some events could be as devastating as watching a cow shed tears before slaughter. It was as if they knew what was about to happen to them, but could do nothing about it. Donata had led me to the slaughter. She had messed up my life as I watched and there was nothing I could do about it.

One time, a rogue elephant at Shimba Hills in Kwale had confronted us during a sunrise nature walk. Our tour guide had shot in the air and the elephant had changed its mind and warded off in the opposite direction, its fat bottoms fast disappeared into the thick forest.

It unnerved one, made one lose confidence and the pleasurable thoughts of sight seeing. It was one of those unpredictable moments in one's journey of life. If you were lucky, you escaped, if not, you got trampled on and that could be the death of you, if lucky enough, you could escape with broken limbs – disoriented, disorganised, and unproductive for the rest of your life. Now that I was alone and hunted, I easily empathised with the lone elephant.

When I first heard tales of cows shedding tears and mooing in pain, misery and protest from my Aunty Bernadette, I did not at first believe her. I laughed it off, making her feel offended. Then, I had discreetly inquired from a butcher friend from where I often bought a kilo of meat for my beef stew. He admitted, albeit reluctantly, afraid I would stop buying meat and he would lose a regular customer.

The matter disturbed me. Was it the way the animals were slaughtered? Could it not be done in a less painful manner? "Well, sometimes they do it less painfully by shooting the cow in the ear."

"But that does not stop the other cows from witnessing the exercise." Aunty Bernadette had informed me. She liked to exaggerate stories and no one believed her even when she told the truth.

Many times, she had been proved wrong and though she was always generous with her apologies, people had come to dismiss her as a joker. Sometimes, one only learnt much later that she had been telling the truth.

It was painful when those you held in high esteem did not believe you. I had approached friends and family to alert them that my life was in danger but they dismissed it all as a figment of my fertile imagination. Everywhere I sought help, I got treated as a crazy woman.

The stigma of being a journalist also hit hard. "You know you are a journalist and capable of creating any story you want. What a fantastic story. Why don't you do a film?" my friend Mary mocked me.

People do not trust journalists. "You are our daughter, but we are sorry we cannot trust you because you are a journalist. Journalists are trained to lie. We see them on television every day, adding spice to facts. Exaggeration is their tool of trade. Are you not the same person who once told us that you were taught at the School of Journalism that a journalist should not have a soul?" relatives frankly told me. These remarks from my relatives and some members of my immediate family deeply hurt me.

I felt hungry as I checked into my room at the Oceanic Sand Hotel, but I was too exhausted to eat. I rushed to the bathroom and felt a sense of relief. My thoughts flashed back to my trip to Mombasa hours earlier. At Mtito Andei, the delicious aroma of *samosas* and hot chicken sausages drifting through the window had woken me from my long reverie. I had impulsively felt like dashing to the bathroom and then eating some hot *samosas* but I was terrified someone might recognise me.

I was quite pressed but I had decided to hold my bladder till I got to Mombasa. I felt safer, even though uncomfortable. I tried to divert attention from my full bladder by concentrating on the Taarab music blaring from the bus's lone speakers. The journey had been long and dreary. I did not feel safe, I wanted to reach Mombasa as fast as possible. Malika Mohamed's songs played softly, soothingly, deeply spiritual.

Malika's songs had a special meaning for me. I had been ejected from the warm comfort of my house, my job, my family, my friends, my dog and cat, into the harsh world of the unknown, into a life of fear, frustration, and discomfort.

Thinking about the past made the journey faster and more bearable. Soon we were in Voi and again, the sweet smell of roast cashew nuts was enticing. I bought several packets at Kshs25 each and dropped them in my pocket. I would eat them later when hunger could wait no more.

Taarab music always brought a smile to my face – it drew both sad and happy memories from my past. Memories of the years I shared a room and deep friendship with the talented television actor and script writer, the late Ashina Kibibi at the University of Nairobi's halls of residence, where we were both students. Memories of the first Taarab night I attended at Fort Jesus while I worked in Coast region. Ashina's death – her body was found dangling from a mango tree outside a medicine man's house in Mtwapa – had left me shocked, devastated.

I was out of the country in Cape Town, South Africa on a special assignment when this happened. I felt sad. I felt I had failed her. If only I had been around, perhaps I would have talked her out of it. If she were alive today, she would have accommodated me in her house, or found me a place to hide among her relatives in Malindi. It seemed as if most of my genuine friends had died – Ashina, Poxi Presha among others.

CHAPTER SIX

Political Games

Taarab songs had greatly featured during the 2007 election campaigns. The battle of political wives took a dramatic high with morbid humour that would have shocked the laughing hyenas of Kabar village into silent frowns.

What was the Pentagon? After successfully defeating the government constitutional draft in 2005, popularly known as "the referendum", the Orange Democratic Movement (ODM) transformed itself into a political party. ODM, then the main opposition party selected Raila Odinga, a Luo from Nyanza, as its 2007 presidential candidate. The incumbent was Mwai Kibaki. The symbol for ODM was an orange and while the government's was a banana.

Besides Raila, then Langata Member of Parliament, the Pentagon comprised of Musalia Mudavadi (Deputy Vice President and Minister for Local Government). He represented the Luhya community of Western Kenya. William Ruto, then MP, Eldoret North, represented the Kalenjins in the Rift Valley, while Najib Balala, Mvita MP, stood for Coast Region.

Norman Nyagah, from the Meru Region in Eastern Province, represented the Kikuyu, Embu and Meru of the Mount Kenya area. The Pentagon was expanded to incorporate Charity Ngilu's National Alliance Rainbow Coalition (NARC) after she broke ranks with Mwai Kibaki. The Pentagon then ended up with six leaders. The Pentagon wives were spouses of the Pentagon leaders.

As some of the Pentagon wives like Ida Odinga, Rachel Ruto, Najaah Balala scrambled for women's votes in Mombasa, Malindi, Watamu, Gedde, Chonyi, Kaloleni Giriama, Changamwe, Ukunda, Tononoka grounds by road, First Lady Lucy Kibaki traversed Faza, Mpeketoni and Kizingitini in Lamu, Malindi, Kilifi, Ganze, Msambweni and Kwale by air.

Journalists on the run all over Coast scrambled for scoops like hungry vultures scavenging for meat. This was our job and we loved it. It was tedious. We lived permanently on the road, took hundreds of pictures but knew only one would go on the page, filed stories over the phone and dashed like a swarm of hunted bees to the nearest town for possible network to download and send pictures. Sometimes there was no network. We jumped into the jeep and dashed yet to another town hundreds of kilometres away to try our luck. Meanwhile, editors in the head office yelled at us in deadline driven desperate voices for quotes and paragraphs over the phone, unaware of the torturous pot holes and dusty rides we wallowed in.

Lucy looked as fresh as a cucumber, with ten shiny silver bangles that matched silver earrings, body stockings and sensible black closed shoes. She had a fresh manicure with red un-chipped nails. The Pentagon wives were, on the other hand, smart in their designer Orange party clothes when they started their campaigns. Somewhere along the way, dust and thirst ambushed them. It was a rugged ride through the rugged dry coastal terrain and bushes.

With a distance of 1500 kilometres to cover, they only occasionally got a minute to grab a sip from their warm plastic water bottles as they waited to address the patient audience. Lucy did not drink any water in public. If she drank a swimming pool of water in the air before she landed, that remained her secret. Perhaps from experience or mere intuition, she had learnt that one did not drink bottled water in front of women who trekked tens of kilometres through dangerous forests full of wild animals to get a scoop of dirty brown water.

Like Lucy, the Pentageese (a nickname coined by some supporters) wore closed shoes, except Najaah, who wore very high-heeled brown open shoes that would have served her well at a salsa dance rather than a political rally. Most of the women at the rallies were poor women and to them, shoes were a luxury. Some had torn, worn out, dusty rubber shoes that had long finished their journey and were only waiting for their final rest. They stared with child-like interest and fascination at Najaah's shoes, like some dwarfs staring at Goldilocks' shoes. They showed more interest in the shoes than on what Najaah was saying.

Pentagoose Tessy Musalia Mudavadi, popularly called Mrs. Mutafat campaigned in Western and Nyanza and did not therefore join her "co-wives", the other Pentageese. Her greetings were however passed on at every stage.

Women came out of the comfort of their huts in some of the largest crowds ever witnessed at a coastal rally. They were curious to see what women of high rank were made of. They assessed the Pentageese as if they were cows or goats for sale at a market day in Ahero in Kisumu. They debated animatedly on what they wore, their beauty and estimated their ages. They discussed whether Ida was older than Raila or if Najaah was older than Balala.

The Pentageese acted prim and proper to a judgemental audience. They must have realised that being a politician's wife had its own consequences. You became public property, vulnerable to any crowd whose vote you sought. They determined whether they wanted you to address them or not. They used offensive language against you but you could not appear angry. You needed them. They did not need you. In Malindi, Pentageese experienced this when illiterate women gave unsolicited advice to Najaah as she addressed them.

"*Wewe Mama, umefanya vizuri sana kuvaa Bui, nguo ya heshma. Ahsante sana Mama kwa heshima zako, Lakini jikaze nawe kama wenzako, upate kukomaa. Pasa sauti, Mama. Usiogiope Mama!*" (You have done us proud by wearing burka, a respectable attire. Thank you for showing us respect. But you need to pull up your stockings in order to be at par with your counterparts. Raise your voice. Don't be shy!)

They showered Rachel Ruto, a skilled speaker, with praise. "*Wewe Mama umeshakomaa. Sasa umfundishe wenzako pia mpatane!*" (You have matured in politics. Now you need to hold the hands of your colleagues so that you can attain the same status.) Rachel is the wife of the Eldoret North MP William Ruto, who was later to become an ICC indictee.

So petty was the gossip in the crowd that they discussed how sexy or otherwise the names were, how delicate their fingers were and which of the Pentageese could do serious farming using a *jembe*, or if their backs were strong and flexible enough to draw water from a borehole.

At one point, the love for Lucy became embarrassing when it turned from respect to deference. The then Kwale MP and minister for Foreign affairs, Ali Chirau Mwakwere, knelt down before Lucy at a rally in Msambweni in his constituency. He sang her platitudes and said, while bowing, "*Mama mpendwa, hata siwezi nikataja jina lako, yaani ile heshima niko nayo kwako Mama, sistahili kuongea mbele yako, hata siwezi kueleza...wacha tu...ama niseme?*" He asked the jubilant crowd. Wacha tu!" (Beloved mother, I cannot even address you by name, I cannot even express the kind of respect I have for you! I'm not worthy to speak before you, Mama or do you want me to express my awe for you? No, I won't! Just let me be!")

He came to the rally with a group of MijiKenda women who seemed to have rehearsed their drama well and knew exactly when to interject. As he uttered these words, the women bowed alongside him with deference, while some lay prostrate on the ground before Lucy's feet. They sang her praises and played drums. It was something out of this world and some of the media houses captured it.

Kwale MP, famous for his song and dance prowess, had not only mastered his artistic skills, he had sharpened his court jester abilities too. I had interviewed Lucy Kibaki before, in the year 2002 in my stint as a Features correspondent at The Nation Media Group in Nairobi. She had just began her tenure at State House and learning the ropes of a First Lady. Lucy was kind, warm, motherly and very patient during the interview.

She talked of her husband President Mwai Kibaki fondly and romantically. "He is a good husband, a good father to his children. He loves them and often enjoys playing with them next to the swimming pool. He also has an eclectic sense of humour and our home is full of laughter," she added.

Lucy praised Kibaki's trumpet skills from his days at Mangu High School. "He really loves Jazz, and we dance a lot." She chuckled with nostalgia about their wedding when she was only 24 years old. Kibaki was surely the love of her life, the love of her youth. Like every woman who is still in love with her husband, she said only very good things about Kibaki. She was the loyal and faithful wife, ready to hold the family together.

"So, your Excellency, what kind of meals do you have at State House?" I posed.

Lucy laughed for a long time, quite amused by the question.

"Oh, we are very natural, down to earth people," she said. "We just eat *githeri* (a mixture of boiled beans, maize, and sometimes potatoes and cabbage), *nduma* (yams), sweet potatoes and porridge. Mzee really likes *nduma*!" she said. It was a few days to Christmas and she looked forward to spending Christmas with her entire family.

CHAPTER EIGHT

Wrong Number

DONATA WAS A WRONG NUMBER. Her actions conjured up deep spirits from my past, buried in my dark historical archives. She reminded me, not just of my days back in college but of my best friend Ashina Kibibi. Then trails of injustice littered the various University campuses, when the highest authority, the office of the vice chancellor remained helpless in dangerous situations.

Ashina and I shared rooms both at the women's hall at the University of Nairobi, officially known as St Mary's and at the prestigious Stella Awinja Hall opposite the Young Women Christian Association (YWCA) hostel for several years before the janitors gave each of us our rooms. I had not known Ashina personally before joining campus, but I had seen her act in the popular TV drama series, "Tausi", on Kenya Broadcasting Corporation (KBC). She was definitely a gifted actor, although acting came with its own hazards as Ashina was to tell me later.

I was in second year at the University when Ashina joined first year. There was a technical hitch and Ashina could not get a roommate. No student wanted to share a room with her – especially after acting on TV with a transparent nightdress that had revealed her underwear on the screen. The day she joined college, there were riots by especially male students who camped outside the vice-chancellor professor Phillip Mbithi's office demanding that Ashina be denied the right to stay in college. She could be a day student if she so wished but they could not stand her presence in the halls of residence.

The rioting students made outrageous claims from the way she dressed to some of the roles she had played in "Tausi". Apart from being the script writer for the series, what had apparently annoyed the rioters was the part she had attempted suicide while in character. It is ironic that Ashina later committed suicide in real life, just like the character she had acted on television.

They alleged the play was low quality, acted in Kiswahili language and would taint the image of the University of Nairobi. They claimed Kiswahili was poor class language and any student at the University should not be allowed to identify with such a language. It was English or nothing! Cartoons and insult-laden graffiti of Ashina appeared all over campus with negative comments. It all seemed crazy. After meeting the vice-chancellor, the janitors called me to their office and requested me to stay with Ashina. They said the VC had asked them to look for a student who was kind and compassionate enough to be Ashina's room- mate. I felt honoured by the compliment and I obliged.

Thus, began our deep and life-long friendship that would pass the test of time. Our families met and got to know each other, we shared family occasions, birthdays, funerals, and holidays. We studied together, cooked our meals together and plotted scripts. We dreamt of one day becoming famous writers all over the world.

She wrote drama, I wrote short stories that were later published in anthologies. We shared the grief of her adopted son, Daddy's sudden death. Ashina had a special love for Taarab music. She played all kinds of Taarab on her small black radio which she had bought with her student allowance.

She would play music continuously all day even when away from the room and all night when she was fast asleep. It was quite interesting the way we studied with the music in the background. It was also interesting how we slept with lights on all night.

Soon, I found myself unconsciously humming some of the tunes and at times sang some of the lyrics as we prepared her favourite black Coastal *iliki* tea. We sang Taarab as we made *mahamri*, chapati and *mbaazi* in coconut with homemade chilli fried with tomatoes and onions. I preferred *ugali* and deep-fried tilapia.

We shared and acquired a taste for each other's meals. Soon we exchanged our Coastal and Nyanza love for music and I became not just a *Taarab* sycophant but singer as well. Some of the Kiswahili lyrics sounded strange to me and too abrasive initially but after some free lessons on the words and meanings of the songs, I was mistress of the game.

My Kiswahili got more fluent. I cleaned up Ashina's English as she did my Kiswahili. We read out our scripts to each other, exchanged ideas and laughed off our grammatical mistakes. With *lesos* tied around our hips we danced *chakacha*, at times forgetting that we were in campus to study. However, life was not all that pleasant for Ashina. Some students continued to bully her. Today, I see them in public offices and wonder if they remember their trails of injustice and why they had not proved themselves human. I wonder if some of their conduct may have driven Ashina to her fate.

Ashina appeared strong and held her head high. She refused to be intimidated even when we woke up to abusive graffiti outside our door or on the walls of the dark tunnel bridging Central Catering Unit (CCU) and the main campus library from the back.

Ashina was not the only one who experienced bullying and outlandish behaviour at the University. One would not have expected bullying at the University – having gone through that experience in secondary school, but there it was in its raw form.

A female student entered the Miss University contest and was beaten up in her room. Her belongings were strewn on the streets on flimsy grounds - she had lowered the image of the University.

According to our colleagues, University students were supposed to portray an intellectual image; display of physical beauty was not in the mix at all. How this gang of wild students we did not know, took it upon themselves to run and control other students' lives remains a mystery to me to this day.

It was obvious some students carried a baggage of wild habits with them to the University from their homes; passing the Kenya National Exams was not necessarily a measure of success. Justice remained elusive in the country's top academic institution. Justice was a façade, intellectual hooligans reigned free yet they were the same people who would take leadership positions in our country. Some would be lawyers, doctors, engineers, lecturers when we graduated. They committed crimes and got away with them.

Some fellow students were an angry, bitter lot, with affinity for unreasonable violence and instinctive animalistic tendencies. They sounded ruthless and thirsty for blood like hyenas hungry for fresh raw meat. They acted like thugs, unable to reason out with other humans. Innocent motorists, about their business and who by bad luck happened to drive past University Way were blinded in consistent riots, stones thrown at their cars and their windscreens smashed because the hot water system in the students' rooms shut down temporarily. Some rioted because the *chapatis* were not the right shape.

Innocent motorists were often roughed up and robbed

because students had allegedly been served flamingos instead of chicken. Some demanded soft drinks to wash their hands in the dining room and not warm water. Sister Anna Gabriella, a nun who had just left St Paul's University Chapel after evening Mass was raped by a group of rioting students along University Way because their Continuous Assessment Test (CAT) had been postponed due to a power blackout.

Sister Anna Gabriella went into a coma and even though she was rushed to hospital, she never recovered from the shock of her nasty experience. She walked stark naked in the streets of Nairobi, talking to herself, a certain madness having turned her captive, the consequence of the wrath of the 'intellectuals', ready to graduate with degrees, masters and Ph.Ds.

Among the favourite *Taarab* music Ashina and I shared were 'wrong number' and 'Ngwinji'. She would enter the room singing:

"Wrong namba, simu bado ni mzima, wrong namba, jaribu nyingine hima, wrong namba, labda anza za nyuma."

The song now reminded me of Ocampo's braggadocio press conferences in which he promised to bring to justice all Kenyan indictees, including several members of Parliament and the police.

Ashina explained that the song was about a woman whose rich lover man was too busy to pay attention to her or pick her calls. He mistreated her to the extent that he would at times pick her calls but pretend she had called a "wrong number", especially when he was in the company of another lover.

The dejected woman was not rich but she dropped the man and got herself a new boyfriend. As luck would have it, her fortunes blossomed and she became a rich and famous musician.

When news of her fortunes reached her ex-lover, he desperately called her number, and tried to rekindle their lost love. Instead, she gave him a dose of his medicine. "Wrong number", she would respond every time he called and disconnected the phone. By then, her ex had lost all his fortunes.

Ocampo and Bensouda had lost most witnesses through careless un-strategic moves and were now desperate in their search as they clung on to the last straw and messed up potential; witnesses' lives. They were wrong number.

In college, we often gossiped about the male students. We labelled most wrong number. Their main agenda, according to our assessment, was to make as many sexual conquests amongst as many female colleagues as possible, leaving them pregnant, devastated and abandoned.

Wrong Number. After their conquests, they sat next to the block adjacent to the Jomo Kenyatta Memorial Library in front of the Department of Population Studies and loudly discussed their sexual exploits. They whistled, mocked and named their conquests loud enough for all and sundry to hear - oh those colleagues of ours! They sat strategically on the route to the lecture halls, and ensured they embarrassed female colleagues and made them rich fodder for sexual scandals.

Ashina and I watched in grave disappointment as our impregnated and abandoned colleagues left our comfortable halls of residence and moved to the slums to rent rooms using student loans.

They started a tough life from the ashes of still-born love. Once in a while, a baby would be born in the halls and the shrill cry of a new born would reveal the well-kept secret and send the mother student packing to the slums. We swore to have nothing to do with these "wrong numbers". "No boyfriends among the 'cockroaches'," we declared. "Cockroaches" was the nickname for the male students with excessive sexual appetite. They hid in the dark and sneaked into the women's halls often in a single file to try their luck.

Wrong Number. They moved from room to room, like moths attracted to bright light. They successfully made dates with several colleagues in one night, drinking lots of orange squash, pretended to go for a short call only to sneak into the next room for quick, passionate romance.

From there they excused themselves, only to sneak into another room for another quick exploit and orange squash. This went on the entire night. In the day, they analysed their nocturnal achievements outside the library, mighty proud of the sins of their youth. Wrong Number.

The University offered unfettered freedom to students who had never really lived away from their guardians or parents; free money, good food, free time and a good life overwhelmed many. Only the self-disciplined survived the onslaught of free sex, lots of beer and wrong friends.

We also added the tag "wrong number" to male colleagues for not taking a shower. They distracted lessons by their nauseous smell but still managed to accurately quote William Shakespeare, Franz Fanon, Malcolm X, Richard Wright, Ibsen, Tolstoy, Chinua Achebe, Ngugi wa Thiongo, Micere Mugo, George Lamming and Francis Imbuga.

We, however, excused those who did not comb their hair. Unkempt hair was a sign of 'intellectualism' as portrayed by most of the professors and our lecturers.

The place seemed more like a sex institution, where students had come for degrees in sexual prowess than academics. Sometimes, these comrades-in-sex picked female prostitutes from Koinange Street and called all their friends. They raped them in turns and beat them up badly.

Many commercial sex workers broke their bones as they jumped out of the window of the men's hostels to escape the tragedy of a pleasurable night turned ugly.

The other roving numbers were our male colleagues who stole tomato sauce, knives, forks, spoons and salt dishes from big hotels like the 680 and Intercontinental. They were people to avoid like the plague. But soon, we added some female colleagues to our list of wrong numbers. Our colleagues, who wore mini-skirts at night and went to parade their wares at the infamous Nairobi's Koinange Street. Female students who were picked from the rooms by our male lecturers and later got 39 out of 40 in Continuous Assessment Tests (CAT) they had not sat for.

This happened as we sat for long hours in the library, reading for some CATs. They edged us out of 1st class distinctions we worked hard towards down to lower second class honours or passes.

As far as we were concerned, these were students without a conscience who with their monkey business opened our eyes to the realities and unfairness of the education system at the university. Wrong number.

Yet we only got to know of some of these cases when an exceptional incident occurred like this case. We had gone to pick our CAT papers from the lecture's office on 3rd floor – Administration Building next to the Dean's office, Faculty of Arts. We suddenly heard shouts.

It was Tito, a colleague's boyfriend, threatening to shoot the lecturer. Tito was dating our classmate Rosa whom he fondly called "heartbeat". He said his love for her was so deep that he breathed with her heart. But word reached Tito that our lecturer, Mr O. had picked his girlfriend from the halls of residence in his old blue Volkswagen and driven with her towards Parklands.

Eye-witnesses, mostly male colleagues, allegedly saw Rosa as she drank cold beer and kissed Mr O. fully on the mouth. The same eye witnesses informed Tito of his heartbeat's betrayal and feeling that he could not breathe anymore, Tito set a trap for the couple.

Tito was sure Rosa had not sat for the CAT that evening. They had both gone to watch a movie, 'Steve Biko' at the C20 cinema hall in city centre. She reminded him about the CAT but Tito had insisted that he could not breathe if she left him.

They both missed the CAT. When we went to pick our CAT marks, Tito was angry that the lecturer had entered 0 out of 40 against his name while Rosa had 39 out of 40.

Tito's discovery happened when he went to request for a special CAT on the grounds that he was unwell when the CAT was written. It took the University Security to save Mr O. from Tito's wrath.

Ashina and I added Rosa's conduct to our list of "wrong numbers". We often laughed hysterically whenever I narrated to her the incident over and over again. Rosa continued with her life and her studies as if nothing had happened. Now, I had added Donata to the list of "Wrong Numbers".

Hours earlier as we approached the Nyali Bridge, the warm ocean breeze welcomed me to Mombasa. The bus driver had coincidentally played Ashina's favourite Taarab, "Ngwinji" composed by Khadija Kopa and Othman Soud, flooding back memories of my late friend and making me sad; a talented young life, cut so short by life's injustice.

Ngwinji is a song that disparages a high end prostitute who is a shameless braggart. She puts on airs and praises herself for her mastery in controlling men. She also says she is popular and famous. She sits in a group and brags how every weekend she lavishly spends using American dollars. She simply denigrates herself yet men do not really love her, they use her instead.

The singer (Khadija Kopa) mocks her and advises her to stop strutting since she has nothing more special than other women. "You time has run out and you are worthless," she is told.

We had such boast cocks in college. They bragged about their parents' wealth but did little to make their own money. We dragged them into the dustbins of 'wrong number'.

Taarab is addictive and I had never gotten over it. The creativity in the lyrics and the sophisticated management of instruments is an enviable and immeasurable work of art. Literature in a class of its own. During my stay in Coast, I attended Taarab night for the first time.

Many women in Coast have a special love for Taarab, yet in some families it is forbidden as I later learnt at the Fort Jesus function. Decent girls from Muslim and Christian families do not attend Taarab functions.

My cousin Caroline had visited me in Mombasa from Kondele and she accompanied me to the function.

East Africa Melodies troupe from Tanzania and the Mombasa hit favourite Khadija Kopa were performing live. There were hundreds of ladies in attendance and a handful of men. It seemed that Taarab was a woman's show. Outside the Fort Jesus entrance, over 100 men in the traditional long white kanzu sat idly, the bright night light only revealing their shadows.

When I asked some of the young women who sold tickets at the inner entrance the cultural meaning behind this, they giggled in conspiratory silence.

"They are not interested in the music. They sit there to monitor if their daughters, wives or girl-friends have sneaked into the function," one lady volunteered the information.

The women did not wear *burkas* at the Taarab night. They alighted from *tuktuks*, in their long beautiful flowing hair and overdone make-up. Their red, purple and blue lipstick shone brightly. Their short skirts revealed fat thighs and clear skin and not a hint of stretch marks; it was hard to tell the difference between mothers and young girls.

The women were dressed expensively – with so much gold that it almost seemed immoral. "Co-wives", as many as four at a go, wore similar clothes and showed off their hips and their gold in a contest of opulence that really had nothing to do with Taarab.

Most of the women chewed *miraa* (khat) and danced seductively and recklessly like they would never dance again for the rest of their lives if they missed this God-given chance. It reminded one of the folktales of the elephant that danced itself lame at a party and stepped on the tortoise, which excreted fire and burnt up everything at the party.

The Taarab queens danced in high- heeled golden shoes and never missed a step, while those gifted with enormous bottoms swayed to the rhythm of the music. They were adorned in golden ears, golden noses, golden necks, golden arms, golden feet – like the fairy tale of the miserly king who wished to turn everything into gold, including his beautiful daughter, Miranda.

I had on my finger an old golden ring which I bought years earlier at a mall to compensate myself after receiving my salary at the end of the month. It had now grown rusty and faded but I was still attached to it – for sentimental reasons. As I watched the expensive display of gold in the room, I instinctively dug my hand inside my faded jeans pocket to hide my modesty. I felt ashamed for my poor finger and made a mental note to adorn it with a better golden ring in future.

My cousin and I laughed over our past and enjoyed Taarab well into the night.

As I slept on my bed at the Oceanic Sand Hotel, I noticed Mombasa had not changed much in the five years I had left. It was as noisy as ever with different Taarab music that drifted out of different households.

My window overlooked the Casablanca International Club and foreign music enhanced by the disco streamed into my room. I once passed outside Casablanca Club every day on my way to and from work for about two years and I knew the activities in there like the back of my hand.

Apart from its questionable nocturnal activities, it served good lunch – fried tilapia fish with sauce and *sukuma wiki* (kales) with well-made *ugali*.

Human deceit, desperation and poverty forced women in burkas to leave their gowns at the entrance next to offices around Kenya Broadcasting Corporation (KBC), with the watchmen, and walk into the club scantily dressed, ready for the intrigues of the night. They mostly targeted sailors and politicians who were hungry for sexual favours.

Sometimes, the Chinese sailors came to Casablanca in a group. They fished for a client who could manage all of them at one go. Like the tailor in the English folktales that had killed seven flies – all at one go. Most of them could not resist this lucrative offer. According to the prostitutes, God helped those who helped themselves and they were helping themselves.

"By the way, our clients include journalists, policemen, pastors, doctors and politicians; let's just say people from all walks of life," the talkative Zabibu confessed.

During my ten-day stay in Mombasa, I longed to revisit Casablanca and eat the fish fry with sauce. But I was in hiding and could not afford to expose myself. Besides, I had little money and I was not sure how I would survive before I got an affordable place to stay. I sneaked out in my newly acquired *burka* and headscarf. I watched my back as I bought some takeaway chapati and beans stew at Kshs30 – my new diet. I also bought a bottle of mineral water and only sipped a bit, three times a day to rehydrate. By the third day, my smooth, clear face had broken into rashes. I knew it was a combination of stress, fear, and lack of adequate water.

I contacted two old friends and asked them if they could give me temporary accommodation. One said she was on her way to Nairobi for a seminar while the other claimed his wife was visiting with her sister and mother-in-law so it was not possible.

I saw fear in their eyes and I understood. Ashina was brave. If Ashina were alive, she would have found a place for me to hide.

I was holed up in my room for the next nine days. I moved between my bed and the bathroom. I wished I could visit Mama Ngina Drive and eat hot chilly crisps as I watched the huge ships dock and leave the port, escorted by smaller ships and boats. How I wished I could go to Nyali Beach Hotel or Travellers Beach and enjoy a glass of wine as the sea breeze embraced my face! How I wished I could walk barefoot on the white sands of the Indian Ocean, dip my feet in the salty soothing water as waves competed to reach the shore! How I longed to watch the beach boys seduce white elderly tourists, dressed in bikini, trying their luck – just in case they caught a rich woman in search of an African man! How I wished I was free! But this was not a vacation. This situation had no name, yet!

It was not only fishermen who cast their nets for a good catch at sea. Beach boys and tourists did too. On a lucky day, it was possible to catch a rich divorced female tourist who needed a strong virile local man for a second marriage.

On a rainy day, the female tourists might catch a beach boy – but only for a one night 'stand. The male tourists, mostly elderly men cast their net far – often catching young, underage girls who had dropped out of school for a dream life with a rich white man – these species were different – they held your hands and kissed you in public and treated you well. They took you shopping and gave you a good life.

My attempts to get accommodation from my old friends hit a rock. It seemed that I had not chosen my friends wisely. If a friend had approached me with a similar situation, I would have taken the risk. I had done it before. I took friends into my house when they had nowhere to stay. But again, this was no ordinary case…few people wanted to get entangled with state agents or ICC matters.

On the tenth day, I looked for a cyber cafe on Moi Avenue and tried to get online and speak with Wolf but I could not get through. I tried Karoli's' email; I could not get through either. Two hours after I left the cyber, I was paralysed to see two state security agents pacing up and down Moi Avenue. I panicked. They had tracked me through the internet. They knew I was in Mombasa. I crossed the road and walked towards Mombasa Village. They seemed not to have recognised me in my *burka* and huge dark goggles. But I was shaken.

I waited until dark then moved, back to my hotel. I packed my bare necessities and checked out. A red *tuk tuk* had just dropped a passenger and I waived it down.

"*Wapi?*" (where to)?

"Mwembe Tayari."

"*Shilingi hamsini pekee, mama.*" (Kshs50 only, mama)," the driver shouted.

I found a bus leaving for Nairobi. I jumped into it and paid Kshs900. I half-listened to Taarab drifting softly from the loudspeakers. I was back to square one. How I wished Nyandwara was still alive. She would have found a place to hide me. She would have hidden me in her granary or her huge pot. She would have hidden me in her smoky kitchen, behind the firewood and nobody would have found me. She would have sent me among relatives in Ombeyi, Kimira or Kamagaga. Or even to Wang'aya, Masogo, Kajulu or Lela or Migingo. How sad it was not to have grandparents!

A home without grandparents is like a broken water pot. It is like a desert. My grandfather Opiyo died long before I was born. My maternal grandparents were both deceased. I had been advised not to go anywhere near home. In the rush to escape, I had forgotten my diary with all my contacts.

I tried to remember some of my friends' telephone numbers but my mind went strangely blank. When I got to Nairobi, I did not know what to do. Still in-flight mode, I jumped into a Mash bus headed for Mombasa again. When I got to Mombasa, I jumped into another TSS Bus and headed back to Nairobi.

In Nairobi, I went down to Nyamakima and boarded a *matatu* heading to Narok. But when we reached Narok, I got into a shuttle heading back to Nairobi. In Nairobi, I got into a bus heading to Kisumu. I was now a fulltime traveller, living in the dangerous killer roads of Kenya. For five days I was on the road, travelling from one part of the country to another, confused.

Passengers behaved badly. They ate as if they were at a food contest, always eating as if that was a fulltime job. They ate bananas, oranges, chips, chicken, *chapati, mandazi,* boiled eggs. I have never understood this special relationship between travellers and eating. It is almost an addiction and with it the consequences; flooded toilets and running tummies.

CHAPTER EIGHT

My Family, My Pillar

THE SUPPORT OF MY FAMILY — my loving Mama and siblings helped me pull through the two months that followed. They pooled their resources and kept me in a safe place. They checked on me daily and brought me food. Little did they realise that they endangered their lives or mine in the process, their anxiety and frequent check-ups on me was a love like no other. Love only a family could undertake.

After I got rid of my phone and of any access to internet, the state agents now trailed my family members — this forced them to relocate me from one place to another as soon as they got wind that my hiding place was about to be exposed.

They prayed for me and came to counsel me. I had watched in horror as Hague witnesses and perceived witnesses went into hiding while IDPs watched the criminals who had killed their families and burnt their homes milking their dairy cows stolen during the clashes.

In Kibera, female victims watched their neighbours who had raped them and their children and evicted them from their homes live in their previous home and walk in their husbands' shirts. Policemen and army men who had been involved in extra-judicial killings walked around freely.

The local cases had flopped due to lack of sufficient evidence. There was no countdown to justice. The police could not investigate themselves. Media blundered by exposing witnesses and safe-houses.

I trembled at the thought that my colleagues might trace me and expose my hide-out. It was indeed a crazy, crazy world. Sometimes, I lived with relatives in places I cannot expose for security reasons. A security agent who had followed me from Nairobi to Kisumu almost deliberately knocked me down as he reversed his car at a supermarket where I wanted to board a taxi. He followed me around town as I sought accommodation. It was slowly dawning on me that I could run but I could not hide. I was disturbed and lost a lot of weight.

I moved to a bar called Timboi where I stayed holed up in a cubicle. It was a new experience for me, sharing rooms with excessive alcohol lovers and commercial sex workers. I had interviewed individuals in the trade before but I had not watched them live.

We shared dirty toilets and bathrooms. I stepped on urine and faeces on the floor. Drunken men and women seemed to have an affinity to throw up. I had no choice but to step on this filth on my way to the loo – for this was my new home, my new life, my safe space.

It was safe to hide here, or so I thought as no one could think of looking for me in such a slimy place. With my status in society as a senior journalist, I imagined that perhaps my pursuers expected to find me in Imperial, Sunset, Victoria or some other hotel of high repute in Kisumu.

Quick sex was the order of the day. Desperate men paid Kshs 200 per room for half-hour to make love with desperate women. Drama was at its best in Timboi. Often a man who had negotiated a sexual deal with a woman would find himself in a fix after the woman disappeared with his wallet.

Most of the young girls sourced milk for their babies; quite a number were underage and after a free beer or two surrendered their bodies for as little as Kshs50. With a good catch, Kshs100 was a pot of gold. Some stole from their drunken clients who beat them and broke their teeth. At times, the flesh vendors whispered over a client who had infected them with a sexually transmitted disease. Syphilis, they said, was the most feared of them all. The smell of stale beer, urine and illicit sex became sweet perfume to my nose. I wanted to live. Timboi was noisy as is every bar with loud music and loud TV – all on at the same time. Oh, the smells and scents my nose would remember if I survived this!

Bleached bar-maids sat strategically, dangling silver beer openers in their itchy fingers. They cast women who walked in with their men hostile spells. It was obvious they wanted the men for themselves and such women denied them potential clients. Still, they were great at the trade and would cause some kind of fracas to their advantage.

The bar-maids were hostile to me at first but soon realised that I was not interested in their men. Then, they suspected I was a government spy because I read lots of old newspapers. After a while, they gave up and left me to my own devices.

"I am very busy. I am a researcher and I have a deadline to write my report. Please do not disturb me or clean my room," I told them.

They smiled in relief. I said little after that. A family member sneaked in books from the home library and I kept my mind occupied with reading. Silence was my weapon.

The ICC and its process had sunk me low – the curse of Donata. I did not want my family to witness this. It was unfair to them, exposing them to such a world of men and women lusty and greedy for survival. They kissed openly everywhere; along the corridors, in the toilets and bathrooms, while some unzipped in public as they pinched their partner's breasts, some as sharp as a razor, some fallen from many years of suckling babies.

Many of the women were poor and only needed money to buy the bare necessities. The constant smoke from cigarettes engulfed the rooms and I thought I would die from suffocation before the state agents abducted me. Smoke from *nyama choma* (roast meat) mingled with cigarette smoke formed a thick pungent mix. Drunkards seemed to have an obsession with roast beef.

Bar-women in scanty clothes sat with their feet on the tables, openly exposing their underwear. The soles of their feet were well scrubbed despite some having been wasted by jiggers in their earlier days and the scars left by the jiggers refused to delete their signatures despite the hard-scrubbing techniques the feet had gone through.

Toe nails that had failed the pedicure test. Their feet were much darker than their arms and faces that had effects of skin lightening creams. Their nails and toes were chipped but painted all the same in red, green or blue. Their hair was the most well-groomed with definite extra care taken with the braids. It was low-class prostitution as compared to Casablanca and as I kept peeping through the windows to check if I was being trailed my eyes took in a lot more than it should have.

Timboi was affordable at Kshs200 a night, unlike Oceanic where I paid Kshs1,100 a night. As an investigative journalist, I was almost tempted to interview the bar girls and the bar owner but this would have exposed me. I watched painfully as a powerful story went down the drain. I had to keep my identity secret and being inquisitive would have raised suspicions. Besides, I was too worried about my safety and writing was the last thing on my mind. I had neither the urge nor the appetite for a story. I read "Chicken Soup for the Soul" and the stories in the book encouraged me, inspired me and gave me hope to live one day at a time.

Occasionally, family brought me newspapers and I kept myself busy as I tried to make the best out of a bad situation.

State agents raided Timboi exactly an hour after my brother, Edu, brought me some food. I had lived there for two weeks and now planned to cross over to the border to Uganda where I would lie low like an envelope. I suspected one of the bar maids may have snitched on me for keeping to myself, all locked up in a dingy room. I jumped over the gate, carrying only my ID and my passport and left everything else behind. I had some money in my purse. I jumped onto a motor cycle taxi as the rain pounded on me. In panic, I did exactly what I had been advised not to do. I headed straight home – to my Mama's house.

Everyone was shocked to see me. I found the door open and ran straight into my Mama's bedroom. I got under the bed – all wet and dripping. Jolawi, my cat, recognised me and started meowing excitedly. My Mama followed me to her room as Edu quickly locked the door. "My Mama, they are after me. They raided my hideout. They were six men. I escaped from the back gate," I whispered, like a cornered animal trapped by the hunters.

"Let us pray," my Mama said confidently as she gently pulled me from under the bed.

"Almighty God, You reign over Heaven and Earth and everything. You created us under your control. We lift You up Oh Lord, we bless You, and we magnify Your name, Oh Holy. Oh, King of Kings and Lord of Lords. Your child has come home Father, with her enemies in hot pursuit, Oh Lord my God. Thank you for protecting her. You know she is innocent Jehovah. You know she has done nothing to deserve this but

You have said that all things happen for the good of those who love the Lord.

"We thank You Father for this test, because You have promised that You cannot give us a burden too heavy for us to bear. Bless Nyaki, Lord. Give her faith, the same faith that her late father and I brought her up in. We know You are on our side Lord. We believe that You will not forsake us. Because You have promised so, in Jesus name, Amen."

Mama gave me a clean white towel to dry myself and some warm clothes. She warned Edu not to admit to anyone that I was there, even if they put a gun to his head. An hour later, after drinking hot porridge and sweet potatoes, she called my other brother Esau and they quietly planned how to secretly get me out of the house. Two strangers had been home only two days earlier claiming they were my friends and asking for my whereabouts. According to Esau, they looked like policemen in plain clothes. I did not want to leave my Mama's house. I wanted to die in my Mama's arms – with my family around me.

I wanted the state agents to shoot me in my Mama's house, where my body could be found and buried next to my late Baba's grave in Muhoroni. I did not want them to abduct me and kill me in the forest, where my body could be eaten by hyenas and I could not be traced. I was ready for the worst. But my Mama became firm and insisted they must move me to another safe location.

I was going to stay with my Mama's cousin, Flora in Ugunja. It was 6.00 pm when I boarded a *matatu* heading to Busia. I was to alight at Ugunja stage and take a motorbike for another 20 minutes to Magoya where Flora lived. I knew her home, having visited her several times before. But I alighted only after five minutes at Kamas and headed back to the bus stop. I took an Easy Coach bus to Nairobi and arrived in my house on Joseph Kang'ethe road at 5.00 am. I got into the house through the back window hoping against hope that nobody had seen me.

I was back to square one, again. At Timboi, they had not asked for my name. No one was interested in anyone's name. Names were private and added no value to the business. There were no receipts either. And many policemen, on the roadblocks to Kakamega next to Junction Inn used Timboi facilities as well – after a hard day's work. But at Easy Coach they had asked for my name, my identity card and my telephone number. It was important for security reasons and to contact one's next of kin in case of an accident. My *buibui* would have helped disguise me but now that I had fled Timboi and left it behind, I covered my face with my Mama's scarf.

There was no food in my house except for sugar and coffee. I had no intentions of going to the shop or exposing myself. For a week, I survived on black coffee, yet I did not feel hungry. I had the working stations in the house and an extra modem. Because I had not seen any one suspicious the whole week, I threw caution to the wind and went on the internet. I could not access my old mail but I opened a new account and sent mail to the CPJ East Africa Coordinator Karoli and my man-friend Wolf in Belgium, informing them I was okay and just indoors. I kept the curtains closed.

The following morning at about 9.00 am, I saw a white car parked outside my house with three men inside. The car was parked side-ways and not in the usual way facing the house. My instincts told me this was strange. I peered through the curtains and watched the men park there the whole day. They looked up towards my house but they did not come out. They seemed busy on their phones. One pulled down the window and I recognised him – the same state agent who had followed me to the shopping centre at Nakumatt Prestige the day I was to meet Donata. What a fool I was, why had I accessed the internet from my house? They had traced me and had now come for me. I remembered the assassination of popular politician J.M. Kariuki, and of Oscar Kamau Kiangara and John Paul Oulu (human rights defenders), shot at point blank range through their car window near University of Nairobi. Witnesses said Kingara was shot four times in the head and Oulu three times. The two men who shot them then jumped into their car and sped off towards the city centre. Eyewitnesses said that an eyewitness at the scene was also shot in the leg and was later taken away from the scene by policemen. I remembered the ICC witness Maina Diambo, shot on Luthuli Avenue a year earlier. I saw the same happening to me. I went to the kitchen window and saw my neighbour throwing rubbish in the common incinerator.

I had briefed her about what was happening and she kept watch for me. The white car drove away at top speed and she alerted me they had left. "I know they will be back. I have to leave now," I told her as I left in a huff. I took a taxi to my sister Catherine's* house in Kileleshwa. She welcomed me with open arms and hid me in her guest room for two weeks. Catherine contacted one Human Rights group and that is how I found myself in my first safe house. If it was not for the kindness I got from Catherine and my other siblings in Nairobi, I cannot imagine what would have happened to me.

I was later moved from one safe location to another, being transferred from one car to another, sometimes four times a day for security purposes and from one part of the country to another. Sometimes when an unmarked car followed us, I would be moved to the boot of a car and covered with a blanket. My first safe house was full of residents but my last one was isolated as I lived alone for about seven months.

At the first safe house, I did not bother to watch TV or read newspapers. Life had taught me so many lessons; that I could survive without TV and newspapers. I could survive without a meal, a mobile phone, and internet. I was still alive although I had not accessed my Facebook or Twitter or WordPress accounts for a long while.

I could not survive without my wonderful family. They loved me without any conditions and I would not exchange them for anything in the whole world. I had had friends in the past, good friends who stuck closer than a brother. Linda Damaris who had offered me accommodation with her mother in Bungoma when I was on the run and endangered her life to make contacts with people who could help me escape. I could have gone to Bungoma. But I thought if the agents traced me there, it would be impossible for me to escape. I did not know the area and I was not sure who the neighbours were or if they could be trusted. My mind was all over and I treated every suggestion with suspicion and unexplained fear.

My dear friend Cynthia Hernandez, down in San Diego, California, who had donated for me blood when I was attacked by thugs after my 'A' levels at Lwak Girls High School and needed 11 pints. She mobilised friends and family as I lay unconscious in the Aga Khan Hospital's Intensive Care Unit (ICU) for months. She would have hidden me in her house.

Friends like the late Vero Kinyanjui and the late Mary Ted who just made life fun despite its challenges and went out of their way to make a difference in one's life. Those friends, had they been alive would have found a place for me to hide.

I turned my anger on God for abandoning me. He was supposed to be my best friend, He was supposed to care for me and sort out my problems. Nyandwara had made many enemies in the village for her raw truth. Friends did not want to be told the truth. They loved people who flattered them. Truth was painful to many. But with God, it was supposed to be different.

I faced God directly with tough, hard questions, like the ones asked in BBC's "Hard Talk." It was time to have an honest conversation with God.

"My Lord, My King, My Master, my Friend! I am completely disturbed. I am confused. I bow at your Holy Feet. I don't know what I want. I don't know what to do. Save me, Lord! I don't even know who I am anymore, Lord. But to tell You the truth, My Friend, I feel as if I am a walking corpse. No one understands what I am going through, what I have gone through in the last nine months. It has taken a toll on me, Father. You have all the power, Lord. Why did you let Donata do this to me?

"I am depressed. I am down, almost out. I feel as if I am going mad. I need someone to talk to. Someone I could pour out my heart to. I feel like a fish out of Lake Victoria, denied a chance to breathe. My Lord, I need to talk to You. I need You to listen carefully, please. I want to tell You everything because I know that my secrets and fears are safe with you. I know you will not bad-mouth me, my Friend.

"Please deliver me from this destructive journey started by Donata and her ICC cronies. I want to go home, to be with my Mama. But this fear of the unknown makes me shake like leaves in the heart of a whirlwind. My thoughts are clouded, Oh Lord. I cannot think clearly. I pray for sanity, my Lord, that I may not lose my step and fall, that I should not give up when I have come this far, just when I am about to reach the end of my journey – when you have walked with me safely this far. Do not abandon me, please!

"Come fast Lord and save my sanity before I go mad. You promised, My Redeemer, that whoever knocks on your door, You shall not turn away. You promised, that whoever seeks an answer from you, shall find it. You promised that whoever asks anything of You, You shall provide an answer.

"Answer me, Lord! I know everyone has given up on me, but Father, you must not do so! For whom else shall I turn to? Who would bear my load, if not you! My mind is in ICU. My mind is *Hagued* Lord! I need a breather. Resuscitate me, Oh Lord. Blow your breath on me, urgently, so that I can breathe freely again. Please forgive me, Father for praying for so long. Please don't get bored with my prayer or feel that I am asking for too much. Thank you my dear Friend for listening. I trust and believe that it can never be too late for you to do something about my situation. In the sweet name of Blessed Jesus, my Lord and Saviour, Lord I pray. Amen."

I believed God was my last hope. He sat at the real court of last resort in Heaven and not the one at The Hague. I needed God to spare me the madness that I saw fast approaching. Madness is not only walking in rags or talking to oneself on the streets. There is madness that captures a solitary mind – the madness of solitude, of being separated from your home, friends and family, from your dog and cat. Madness that comes out of loneliness. Such deep sorrow that made one's heart ill that gave way to madness. I invoked the name of sanity. "Lord, take away everything from me, as you did to Job, but please let me keep my sanity. Amen!"

My voice trembled with emotion whenever I spoke. My voice shook in fear, anger, pain, and bitterness. I was afraid of today, I was so afraid of tomorrow, I was terrified of yesterday – of all that had happened and could happen.

After my long conversation with God, I felt better. I blamed Donata and the ICC for my predicament. I acted like a victim, stuck in one place unable to get on with my life, waited for Donata to pay for my tragedy. I was drunk with fury and anger. I did not want to play victim anymore. Things had happened and disrupted my life. But it was now time to take responsibility for my future. My destiny was in my hands.

These were great lessons from the past and that was why one had to be wise when dealing with strangers. Donata was a stranger to me when she called. But like the hyena hungry for meat, she had recklessly and carelessly exposed my life to danger – then turned her back on me – claiming she had wanted to have a conversation with me but now she was no longer interested. She had gobbled up my life, my career, ruthlessly like the hyena, in what she believed was her pursuit for justice.

Doubts had been raised in the local media about the credibility of the International Criminal Court. I silently added my doubts to the list of protesting voices. My faith told me that the court of last resort was in Heaven where everyone would be judged equally at the feet of God the Father – and nobody would be superior to the other, or use their Hague powers to mess up others.

CHAPTER NINE

Back to Square One

WHILE I HID AT MY SISTER CATHERINE's house in Kileleshwa, she remained in constant touch with various human rights organisations, my lawyers, the Committee to Protect Journalists, the UN Human Rights Office in Gigiri and the Kenya National Commission on Human Rights. Meanwhile, she made arrangements to have me transferred to a Safe House. Life in Catherine's house was not easy as I remained confined to the bedroom upstairs. I was to remain as quiet as a mouse whenever she had guests in case someone got a hint I was here. I could not draw the curtains. I had lots of magazines and books to read, but I could hardly concentrate on what I did. She instructed the house help to bring me food to my room. In the evening, when she came back from work, she would sit with me and counsel me, often urging me to be strong and not to give up hope. She brought me greetings and messages from my family. We also read the Bible and prayed together.

She claimed she sometimes saw her car followed by strangers and she was fearful that they could trace me at her place. She asked me to have my belongings packed and ready as I could be picked up any moment and transferred to an unknown destination. "It could be Europe, Uganda, Tanzania or South Africa," she said.

I waited anxiously for three weeks, unable to stare out of the window. Then one day, Catherine showed up from her workplace at midday and told me to get into a taxi that waited outside. She said she followed instructions from Human Rights officers and I must be as co-operative as possible no matter how much discomfort I felt.

"Cover your entire face and head with a black scarf. Here are some dark goggles. Put them on. No earrings, make up or bangles! As you approach the car, do not look left or right. Get in through the back-left seat and lie flat on the car seat. I will cover your whole body with a blanket. Pretend that you are luggage! Do not move even if you cannot breathe. Do not make any sound!" The instructions came fast and furious. She was panicky and so was I.

We left Kileleshwa in whirlwind speed but on the Chiromo Lane, next to the Chiromo mortuary, we realised an unmarked white car was following us. When the taxi driver stopped, the car behind us stopped. The driver turned left towards Westlands and sharply turned into a petrol station next to the Consolata Shrine. The car followed us into the petrol station. "There are four people in the car behind us," Catherine told the driver. She sounded worried. "Please find a way to lose them." Meanwhile, Catherine called another taxi parked outside Waumini House in Westlands and asked him to come over to the petrol station, but not to enter inside. She then called two of her male friends and asked them to wait for us at the main bus stop before the Westlands roundabout.

Our taxi swerved towards Westlands and in between the heavy traffic jam around the Westlands roundabout, Catherine jumped out of the taxi, opened my backseat door and pulled me out into the other taxi. She seemed to have strategized well for the taxi arrived with two bulky mean looking men, one said to be a pastor of a church. I sat between the two men and we headed off towards city centre - the highway was safe, Catherine advised. Meanwhile, she constantly called the Human Rights security officers who guided her to take me to the All Saints Cathedral Church opposite The Serena Hotel. She called the driver whose car we had just left and he said he had branched off towards Parklands as the strange car had followed him, until he lost them near MP Shah Hospital.

At the All Saints Cathedral on Kenyatta Avenue, we parked outside the gate and moved yet into another car. Finally, we got to the Human Rights office in Lavington. Here, I was switched to yet another car and given a protection officer. That is how I ended up at the first safe house, somewhere in the outskirts of Nairobi. This is where I met Dama and her five children and all the other housemates who were to become part of my new family.

This was my first safe house among others that were to follow. The safe house was managed by two women staff known as the aunties. We later learnt they were called Martina and Martha. They served as matrons, cooks, nurses, housekeepers and counsellors. They watched over us like hawks, wrote reports about us and handed them over to the human rights officers, who then determined whether your physical and mental health and conduct would grant you a relocation pass to an asylum country. The aunties did they know our real names.. Everyone in the house was under a witness protection name for security purposes. Everything appeared secretive and everyone talked in whispers. They aunties rarely talked to us and only when necessary. Although The aunties warned us there were very harsh dogs outside, I did not see any, neither did any of my housemates. Security officers exchanged guard day and night. We did not talk to them. We were not allowed to interact with them at any point.

The place was a three-bedroom residential house with a small kitchen, two bedrooms one for women only and others for females and male children under 13. I found myself sharing the room mixed with children because the female only room was crowded. The bedrooms were squeezed with triple decks so we could all fit in. It reminded me of the dormitories in boarding school, only these rooms were smaller. We were about 13 housemates, fighting over food, washrooms, airing spaces for clothes, chairs in the living room and hot water in the chilly mornings.

Breakfast was at 7 am then the Aunties asked inmates to volunteered to do dishes, clean up the house, arrange old newspapers or whatever work was available to keep our minds occupied. If there was no work, they created some like scrubbing bathrooms, walls, windows, verandah, scrubbing huge *sufurias* or cleaning the fridge. The aunties went out shopping for food, prepared lunch and dinner and sat watching television. If no one volunteered, the aunties assigned us duties. We were afraid of the aunties because of the power they wielded. Their word was law and they held our fate in their hands. They let us watch television till 6.00 pm. We were all in bed by 7pm, ready to be bitten by mosquitoes. Some days they were kind, some days they were harsh, it all depended on their mood. We felt like prisoners, caught between the mostly militant aunties and the heartless world outside.

,At the safe house, each new arrival came with a deep problem. It made one's own problems light and shifted attention from one's worries. Although everyone was supposed to keep their problems secret, in minutes, everyone knew the other's problem. Even though the aunties were sworn to secrecy, they too talked. For the victims , it was a way to relieve their burden, to bond and team up in solidarity and defiance against the unties who managed the house, often believed to be unjust, heartless and cruel.

According to Bertha, 14, everything donors had sent filled the store (packed to capacity with eggs and blue-band) but he unties allegedly used them for their own families. How else would one explain the absence of eggs, fruits, rice, etc., in the diet? Why was there no milk for the children?

The unties argued that there were no special favours – even for the sick that were on ARVs and needed to eat well. Most female housemates were HIV positive, having been raped by their fathers or at refugee camps where they sought refuge after civil wars in their countries.

Some were survivors of rape by police, others by neighbours, unknown persons or their own biological or step parents. There was not enough food – not even for Ivy who had undergone a surgery and still had 18 stitches in her tummy. Not even for the pregnant children who now had the privilege of three scarce meals a day after being mistreated and denied food by their own mothers for days on end. If these children had been denied milk by their own mothers, it was illogical, therefore, to introduce milk and other such luxuries in the safe house.

The aunties bragged that the safe house was heaven and that judging by individual's' history and future (which they could foresee), we now had free running water from the borehole, whereas in our future lives we could be fetching water from a long distance. Instead of electricity, they warned us, we could be using lamps or lanterns. "We are only preparing you for the future, for your own good. That's why there is no need to boil water for you to drink. Your future may be a lot worse!" The unties reminded us at every opportunity. I was terrified. I had never drunk unboiled water. I saw myself getting ill of cholera, typhoid, amoebic dysentery and other water borne diseases. I had always lived a privileged life, taking mineral water. I watched all this tumbling down like the walls of Jericho.

The girls were generally rebellious to the rules in the house. Some in their adolescence mixed with the injustices meted on them by society incited the rest. They felt their rights were being violated by the strict house rules and they lacked freedom to have a say in their lives. Most were here under protection from criminals who had caused them harm. Some had to attend ongoing cases in court. Housemates fought over simple duties like sweeping, cleaning, and washing plates. Surprisingly, everyone enjoyed cooking because it meant tasting some food and stealing a few things from the kitchen.

Sharing toilets was not fun. They were dirty and poorly used. I avoided the toilet for as long as I could, until I was so pressed that I would run and close my eyes for business.

Ivy's group of classmates raped her despite her epilepsy, according to the aunties. She had an eleven-year-old child but she claimed she was 19. The dates just didn't seem to add up but the fact was that at some point her male classmates had raped her in turns and impregnated her. She did not know who the father of her child was. She was raped a second time and now lived with her four-year-old son, Baby Boy, at the safe house. She still did not know who raped her. She claimed it happened when she was asleep after an epileptic attack.

Now she was at the safe house after a third rape by four policemen. She said they raped her in turns and threatened to kill her if she reported the matter to anyone. Fortunately, she remembered them and could identify them easily at a parade. She did not conceive this time around, but she was zero positive. Roommates claimed she was a lesbian but she claimed she was bisexual with the male part being more pronounced. Bertha, one roommate who shared the room with her begged the aunties to let her move into the girls' room, but it was full. She vowed she did not mind if she had to move with her mattress.

She begged to sleep on the floor rather than share a room with Ivy. She, however, refused to say what the problem was.

Bertha soon reported to the aunties that Ivy had touched her inappropriately and addressed her as "her" wife. She also alleged that Ivy had also declared all the females in the house "her" 'wives'. The matter was reported to the counsellors and when they stripped her naked, they found she was entirely female with only female organs. They also found a little surprise. An artificial male organ she had planted strategically on top of her vulva made with pieces of cloth and torn underwear. The aunties clarified that she was lesbian and wanted to liaise with the female inmates..

When asked to explain this, she grew hysterical and cried floods of tears. She maintained a two-day silence. The aunties confirmed why she wore boxers and refused to take them off. We now understood why she wore a male cap. The intrigues at the safe house did not end. The stories, all alleged to be true, sounded like fiction. But who did not know that real life often was stranger than fiction?

There was Daudi, the street boy who witnessed a crime by policemen on the streets of Nairobi. They later on realised he recognised them and the police killed his best friend, whom they mistook for Daudi. He was rescued but the 13-year-old did not seem to realise the kind of danger he was in. He was difficult, a bully, a thief and often escaped from the safe house through the fence. He caused concern and worries among the staff and got the guards into trouble for carelessness. The aunties earned a bigger portion of the blame for failed duties. Daudi was street-wise and knew his rights. He was rather wild, often beat up fellow housemates and broke as many rules as he could. He was what you call a 'bad influence" but the aunties feared him and let him get away with murder.

He was untouchable and a valuable witness and had to be

handled with kids' gloves. He was often traced to Kawangware chewing bhang and sniffing glue. That was his life before all these inconveniences happened to him and, as he told everyone, no one would lock him up like chicken in a pen. He helped feed the chicken but demanded instant pay for his service.

According to the Aunties, sworn to secrecy, the prosecutor had made a big mistake in telling Daudi that once he had given all the required evidence, he would be a free man and was no longer needed. With a little incitement and encouragement from the housemates, Daudi was advised that the safe house was only using him to get funding.

When I left the safe house, Daudi had disappeared with Ivy's new sports shoes. I recalled the day I reported to the safe house. He came close, assessed me, then gave me his hand.

"I am Daudi, who are you?"

"Tumi" I said. Since I had given myself the name "Tumi" as I registered at the Oceanic Sand Hotel in Mombasa, I was getting more used to pronouncing it. It did not mean anything. It just cropped up when the receptionist had asked for my name.

"Welcome," he said, smiling as he looked keenly at my belongings.

I do not know if he could have stolen anything of mine, but I had left everything in the Aunties' room, only keeping my toothbrush, the dress I had on and my fur coat. Nairobi was experiencing one of its coldest seasons.

I did not ask for any special favour and stuck to the rules. I did not even know how long I was going to be there. According to Ivy, they lied to you that you would be there for a few days but it could take months. She had been there for two months already when they had told her she would only take 48 hours in the safe house. "They only do that to make you keep hoping so that you do not get disoriented."

I wished she had not told me that since that had disoriented me even more. I took pity on myself. By the fourth day, I reluctantly and painfully resigned myself to my new home. I felt as if I was in a movie; from the comfort of my self-important prestigious life to communal living.

The words of the Human Rights officer replayed in my head. Her last words of advice as we drove to the safe house were, "Be patient. There is a lot of bureaucracy involved but you must be very patient. The minimum time here is 48 hours but if it goes to a week, don't give up. Be patient." I clung to those words as if to dear life.

To fit in, I had to take advice from my guardian and not tell them my story. It was for my own security. I knew if I whispered to one soul, word would soon go round. You could tell by the heightened curiosity, the looks. The extra lengths they went to be friendly. I had to think fast. Most of the cases here were of those of children who got raped by their biological fathers and neighbours, boys sodomised by fathers, mistreated and dehumanised by their own mothers, denied food, young girls withdrawn from school and brought to Nairobi city to be house girls, only to be thrown into the streets by cruel female employers, and women battered by their husbands.

The housemates waited impatiently for two days. When they failed to hear a word from me, they volunteered their stories, one by one. I did not fall for the trick.

"Looking at your clothes, jacket and suitcase, you seem to be from the affluent side of the society. What happened? Did your husband rape you and throw you out of your beautiful home?" they inquired. I kept mum.

The level of sympathy elevated to a new level. The housemates grew kinder, got me food and asked to do duties on my behalf. They advised me to ask the aunties for some piriton. "If you take two at night instead of one, you will definitely sleep." I did that and slept well but failed to wake up in time for my toothpaste and warm water. I had two tubes of toothpaste in my suitcase, but the house rules would not allow me to use them. I went to the kitchen, grabbed some salt and gurgled as I cleaned my teeth with the toothbrush. The tap water was cold but I bore it. I then went and had my lukewarm bath. I only washed my face and feet. But the following morning I woke up sneezing and knew I was down with flu. The aunties only gave me two tablets.

Meanwhile that toothpaste issue made me resent the aunties. I started viewing them as oppressors, heartless and ruthless and lost any little respect I had for them. I soon joined the resentful housemates in solidarity and gave them a few tips on survival. One did not need toothpaste in the morning. Salt killed all mouth bacteria, reducing mouth infections. The team hung onto my words without question. I was, after all, much older than them in terms of age and experience. My advice, though useful, took an unexpected turn. Roommates ignored the official 6.00 am wake up time when a pinch of toothpaste was distributed on everyone's finger and slept till late.

They all went to the kitchen and took some salt for the exercise. Little wonder then that the hawk-eyed aunties soon noted the strange behaviour and hid the salt. The traitors snitched on me. The aunties glared at me ferociously but did not say a word to admonish me. They had no reason or excuse to do so. I tried my best to stick to the 6.00 am program and never missed my toothpaste again. To appease them, I volunteered to do the most hated duties – cleaning the carpets and straightening the table clothes at 6.30am, and washing utensils after every meal. Scrubbing *sufurias* spoilt my nails but such was life. They were surprised.

"You don't mind the cold water?" Aunty Martha asked.

"No," I said. Washing dishes is my hobby. Besides, it keeps me busy and helps me forget my agony and worries."

To test my hobby, Aunty Martha removed all parts of the huge fridge and freezer stained with food and dirt for me to wash. I did so obediently.

Soon I was in the aunties' good books, but only for a while. I took two cups of porridge against the house rules. I took it defiantly with the help of Mama Dama, the new entrant in the scene and Faith, the refugee who had spent 20 years in Dadaab Refugee Camp in North-Eastern Kenya. Dadaab houses over 600,000 refugees from the war-torn countries of Congo, Ethiopia, Somalia and Sudan.

Aunty Martina, one of the aunties in the safe house later confessed that they were surprised by my adaptability at the house. Jay had told them that the client they were bringing to the safe house was "high tech" and she looked like she would even ask for a duvet. It now explained how the Aunty had come asking me meanly if I wanted a blanket. She sounded like she was spoiling for a fight yet I did not understand why. It now made sense. She had expected me to ask for a duvet and she seemed to have prepared for a confrontation. I gently said I had no blanket but it was okay. I would use my warm fur coat. She pulled out a blanket from one of the wardrobes. I said thanks and spread it down underneath the sheets. My warm fur coat kept me comfortable despite my sleepless nights. Still, I murmured a prayer for the aunties for the sacrifices they made to keep us safe.

I shared a room with young boys aged four to ten who wet their bedding. The aunties would not help them air or wash the bedding. It was everyone for themselves and God for us all. The bigger boys aired their wet blankets, mattresses and sheets on the wet grass outside the cold chilly Nairobi 'winter'. But the younger boys like Toti and Bindi were ashamed and hid their wet clothes and bedding under the bed. The room smelt terrible and suffocated one like a public toilet. I offered to assist the small boys carry their heavy mattresses to ease congestion in the room. I also advised them not to be ashamed as this was a mere growing up process.

As I acclimatised to my new strange environment, life went into disarray the moment Dama arrived on a Friday evening with her five children. It was my third day in witness protection. The safe house underwent a complete metamorphosis. She had a one-week old baby and both looked emaciated. They cried at the same time. Baby Banda cried endlessly and tried to suckle the mother's breast in vain. Frustrated, her cry grew hysterical. Everyone was depressed that evening. Even Bertha and Clara who had excessive appetite would hardly touch their food. This Dama, only 25, with five children so closely spaced that they seemed to follow one another by about a year stirred chaos!

The children looked hungry, lost, miserable, poorly kept and unfairly born into this world. They all had protruding bellies. As housemates absorbed the drama, the children soon forgot their problems and started playing. They ran around the chairs and rolled on the carpet to everyone's dismay. The house rules were strict on the carpet. The aunties wanted the carpet clean and no one was allowed to jump on the chairs. As the new guests jumped up and down the seats like naughty baby monkeys and squirrels, the other children – for whom similar behaviour was forbidden – looked at them enviously and soon followed suit, daring the aunties with their side glances to stop them. In a few minutes the fun was over as two of the children pooped on the carpet and seats, spoiling the comfort and new-found happiness. Dama slapped Pity, the older child, then lifted each one with one arm and dashed with them to the bedroom. She left trails of litter on the floor along the way.

The aunties looked confused. The house rules did not allow them to beat the children. All housemates were property of the state. But this was too much. Everyone seemed dumbfounded. Bertha spoke first. "Welcome mama, but in here children are not beaten." Suddenly the aunties talked at once.

"Yes mama, it is against children's rights to bear five children at your age," Daudi found his mouth too. "You are only supposed to beat them on the legs with a small stick. Be careful or they will warn you through the aunties."

Clara agreed, swinging the new-born baby. "If you beat the children again, the aunties will take them away from you and they will be taken to other homes. And you will not have any children left. Be very careful."

But mama Dama was defiant, aggressive, and confrontational. She laughed loudly and spoke harshly. "Nonsense, who says I cannot beat or punish my own children? Did you give birth to them? Nonsense! Stop speaking nonsense!" She dropped the two children in the special toilet meant for the Aunties only to re-appear and ask for a rag.

Bertha, seeking attention because she had not had a chance to carry the new-born baby, had already rushed with the mop and a bucket of soapy water. "Here aunties," she said politely, smiling as if eager to win mama Dama's approval. There seemed to be a kindness, a conspiracy, a liking towards her.

Dama's positive defiance was an asset. She could stand up to the aunties. She could be a reliable ally in any rebellion or go slow for that matter. As the Aunties cleaned up the mess, she stopped for a second, knocked Gloria, 6, her first born's head for no reason. She harshly ordered her to go wash the children. Gloria dashed to the room wailing, washed the children and beat them up in the process. It was a chain reaction of sorts. The mother beat her impulsively and she beat the children for no reason and that, for her, was life, fair and square.

"I am tired! I am tired! I am fed up!" Gloria said loudly, arms akimbo as she washed the children, loud enough for everyone to hear. At six years, she had assumed the full responsibility of being mother, maid and baby sitter to her four siblings. Her language, her mannerisms and general behaviour was like that of an adult. Her voice was as powerful and loud as her mother's. She was an adult in a child's body.

Throughout the evening, she bathed all the children, fed and dressed them before bed. In the process, she lamented as loud as possible. Her mother ignored her. Gloria put her arms akimbo as she stood in the corridor. Her mother had just called her to take the baby. "I am tired, yawa! I am so tired! I am tired of carrying the baby all the time, so tired."

At age six, she had not started school. Gloria confided in me that her father was mean and could not support her financially. She told me that her father had refused to take her to school even though he had money. There are instances, she said, when her father would send her to buy him soft drinks but he couldn't give her a shilling to keep.

"You are lying," I told her, gesturing towards her and wiping tears from my eyes with the back of my hand. We ended up laughing helplessly for a long time. Conspiracy makes good friends. I knew I had earned a friend and much more information was on the way. But before she could say more, her mother called out to her to go and clean the floor where the children had spilt porridge. Gloria was either carrying Dolly on her back or the new-born sibling. She often talked of her father and how he had denied her a chance to go to school. I told myself, if only! If only I could convince Dama to take this brilliant little girl to school! If all this was over, perhaps I could sponsor her education.

Dama was weak, having just delivered Banda a week earlier. Being kind to her children made her open up to me. She volunteered the story of her life without my probing. She was busy washing clothes and Clara had disappeared and was not in the swings, having abandoned the baby on the bed. Baby Banda started crying and I got up from my bed and carried her. I gently swayed her in my arms as I danced slowly around the squeezed room, singing a lullaby:

> *Sleep baby sleep,*
> *good baby sleep,*
> *drinks milk - sleep,*
> *mum is coming - sleep,*
> *she brings bananas - sleep.*

I could not sleep for the next few days. Dama and her clan had converted the house into a noise factory. The children cried most of the night. They cried in their sleep. They cried in their dreams. The new- born cried throughout the night, hungry, yearning for milk – but not a drop, from the mother's dried up tits.

Lord, it seemed like a nightmare yet it was all so real. I was having sleepless nights before the Dama clan arrived, anyway – but quiet creepy nights. I was still traumatised at the turn of events in my life and still could not come to terms with the state my life had come to. I had at first been shocked that I was sharing a room at all, then the additional – not just sharing a room with an epileptic young girl and her son, but three orphaned boys too. I watched the young girl have epileptic fits as she fell from her bed to the cold floor. I ran to the aunties for help only to be completely ignored.

But if I thought that was already too much for my system to absorb, then I was in for more shock. Now we shared the room, 12 of us. If the urine had been filthy, then the pungent smell now clouding the room with the new arrivals could not be described in words. At least one of the comforts I had in the house was the bed. The aunties had warned me on arrival that some of the housemates were suicidal. I tried, therefore, not to be close to anyone.

I often thought of Donata and how she had changed my life completely. I felt angry that she had brought my life to a standstill as she went on with hers as usual. The huge six by six metre bed was comfortable despite sleep being elusive. The aunties had given me a new pair of sheets, a blanket and a new mosquito net. But now that mama Dama had arrived with her clan, I was asked to move to a double-decker bed. I had not slept on a double-decker since my childhood. It did not matter where I slept anyway. Even if I slept on the floor, I would not have felt it. I was already too traumatised to sleep. I spent the night worrying over my problems, afraid for my future, afraid of tomorrow, afraid to die.

When sleep sneaked in, I had nightmares. Policemen surrounded the place – all looking for me. I jumped through the window and escaped. They still pursued me. I woke up, my pillow flooded in sweat. I wanted to sleep. I needed to sleep. I would have paid anything to have my sleep back. When I looked in the mirror that morning, I failed to recognize the face in front of me. I had aged by 30 years in a few days.

In another nightmare, a huge snake chased me across a forest. My feet were paralysed. I screamed but no sound came out. Just when the snake was about to bite me, I woke up sweating. I could not tell which was more dangerous; the nightmares or real life. I wondered how much longer I would survive this ordeal. I retraced my life's footsteps and the sins I had committed to make God look at me so unfavourably. What had I done in my previous life to make God punish me this way?

Our two housemates – Faith and Mercy – the refugees who had spent 20 years at the Daadab camp, gave me hope. I marvelled at their resilience.

In my normal life as I once knew it, I would have left the mosquito net for Mama Dama and her children but the experiences had changed me. I moved with my sheet and blanket and net. The mosquitoes would feast on the children but I was not ready to be the sacrifice. I was afraid of malaria – that dreadful illness that paralyses the bones, makes them weak, causes fever and gives headache. The net did not fit well on the new bed so I basically covered my face well but by morning, I had huge bites on my face and arms.

I soon struck a rapport with Antipas. He slept on the upper bed. He asked me what tribe I was and I said "Luo."

"Oh my God," he said contemptuously. "Luos and stones! You people only know how to use stones; you are cowards, afraid of *pangas*. I know how to use a *panga* better than any Luo man. All you people could use during the post-election violence was stones."

I stared at him in absolute disbelief. I had problems with this strange life in a safe house, all because of post-election violence and the ICC. I had not realised how tribalism and post-election violence was so deeply rooted that an 11-year old boy could chide me over my tribe. I did not expect to encounter tribalism and the effects of that at the safe house.

I looked at the boy and quietly told him, "Antipas, you have no reason to despise me because I am Luo. We are all equal in the eyes of God. He created us all in His image."

"I am sorry," Antipas said apologetically.

"It's okay," I said. But deep in my heart his confrontational verbal diarrhoea had affected me and I tried to keep as much distance from him as possible. It seemed that the curse of Kenyan elections was with us. It touched on every Kenyan and made us lose our minds and common sense. It made us silly. The curse of the Kenyan elections made grown men act like babies and professionals like fools. The curse of the Kenyan elections made violence look like child's play and cemented tribalism deep inside the bone marrow. The curse of the Kenyan elections was right here at the safe house and there was no escaping from it.

There were moments of fun. Every morning after breakfast we enjoyed devotion time. The aunties kept away and we were left to ourselves to sing, dance, share each other's feelings and pray. Housemates sang their hearts out as if the world was ending. Small children gave such powerful testimonies that would have put adults to shame. But there was one universal plea to God: that He should remove us from this safe house and we should join our families and reclaim normal lives.

Most of the residents at the various safe houses were eye witnesses to one crime or another. What made them different from the rest of the public was that their lives were threatened by suspects or their relatives after learning that they had agreed to co-operate with the court and give evidence. Government agencies, human rights watchdog groups, humanitarian organisations against rape and domestic violence referred their clients here for safety.

We were under different witness protection agencies, both local and international and were all being counselled for trauma. Some had witnessed their parents kill each other, their siblings or even attempt to kill them. Some were raped by their parents, neighbours, teachers, doctors or guardians. There were widows and widowers who were sexually abused by their brothers and sisters-in-law. Little girls who were lured into the city by relatives for a better education and were later turned into house helps were all here waiting to be delivered safely back to their parents or to children's homes. We were all here, protected against a cruel society, ready to relocate to a foreign land or other parts of Kenya to try our luck. There were refugees who were sexually assaulted in refugee camps and waited to be transferred to foreign countries to begin a new life.

The safe houses had several bedrooms inside, adjacent cubicles, shared bathrooms and toilets and a common dining room, living room and kitchen. It was shabby and dark. The walls were highly fenced with electric wires and most of the time the residents were only allowed in the backyard for a few minutes. Most of the times, we stayed in the living room, cleaned up, slept, read old newspapers or magazines, plaited hair, or chatted. Television times were restricted between 4pm and 6.30pm. Dinner was at 7pm, after which we were expected to be in bed.

Wake up time was 6 am. We brushed our teeth, had a bath, cleaned the rooms and had communal breakfast, at 7am. All meals were communal. Breakfast was a cup of tea and two slices of unbuttered bread. Lunch was at 1pm – mostly white cabbage and *ugali*, rice or githeri. Dinner comprised *githeri* or white cabbage and *ugali*. Meals were monotonous but once in a blue moon, chicken stew and *ugali* could suffice. The house was abuzz with activities. Witnesses moved to and from court to give evidence, injured residents attended clinics or got P3 forms, traumatised residents saw psychiatrists, and new residents were inducted into the programme. Journalists whose lives were threatened for exposing corruption in government or other sensitive political stories were at the safe houses too.

The time-frame for being in the safe house was two days to one year. If one was lucky, one could move out fast. Some court cases took up to five years or more, so the witness would be moved to a rental house from where they would be picked and secured for court sessions. Some individuals at the safe house were emotionally scarred and needed a long time to heal. They could stay in the safe house for two years or more. Abused children, or those abandoned by their parents, could spend several years at the safe house while awaiting adoption or to be placed in an orphanage, foster care or a school. This could take years too. The safe houses survived on the good will of donor funding, government, faith-based institutions or individual sponsors. Kenyan families donated clothing, blankets, shoes and other necessity items.

At the end of their stay at the safe house, witnesses are inducted into a new life and independent living, assisted to start up a business, or helped to get a job. They would be financed for about six months, have their rent and bills paid by the agencies before being left on their own.

Those who changed their minds about being witnesses and opted to leave the safe house voluntarily were allowed to leave but would not be given any money to assist them. House rules were strict and those who broke them and got in touch with their friends or relatives, thus endangering themselves and other housemates, were thrown out of the safe house and were not assisted in any way to move on.

CHAPTER TEN

Tough Questions

I WAS MOVED TO THREE OTHER LOCATIONS after leaving the first safe house. At one location, I spent one night, and three days at another. Then I was moved to another safe location for two weeks.

My handlers paid me discreet visits, sometimes every day, at times they disappeared for a week or two to ensure no one tailed them. I did not know most of their names. There was no need to. It was safe that way. I saw different faces whenever they visited but I had to trust them with my life. I asked no questions and they volunteered no answers. But they smiled gently, reassuringly and gave me a warm bear hug. The house was stocked with food, groceries, and a cooking place so all I had to do was prepare it.

My handlers, another group of protection officers, handed me over to yet another protection agency, which moved me safely to a lone safe house, far from the city centre. I stayed there for seven months out of touch with anybody. Witness protection rules did not allow me to make any phone calls or access the internet or talk to strangers. "You are your own best security," the protection officers kept hammering this message into my head.

My heart pounded with joy as I went to meet a family representative under the protection of my handlers. In the other safe houses I had lived in, I was not allowed to have any contact with the outside world. My excitement knew no bounds as this was a first. I was going to meet a family rep in a long while. I wanted to dance in the car but the space was too small. The officers warned me from the beginning that our relationship was purely professional and they preferred to keep it at that level. It was lovely to meet a close member of my family. We were too excited to talk. We both gasped for air before she found her voice.

"How are you?" Family rep asked several times, overwhelmed with emotion.

"I am fine," I responded. "But I feel very isolated, I feel so alone," I responded. I stifled my tears and quickly recollected myself.

I introduced my handlers to her and we got a quiet table at a private corner. My handlers were very kind and I must give them credit for treating me with dignity and compassion. Then the tough questions began. My family was concerned and sent a representative to question my handlers on my fate.

How long was this protection going to last? How did you ensure the potential witness was safe? Was she a witness? If she was not a witness, how was she going to go on with her normal life? How did you assess the threats, or rather the level of threats? The answers were not straightforward or forthcoming.

"We are still investigating. We are still waiting for the witness list," my handler responded.

"When is that?" Family rep probed.

"We don't know yet. If she is a witness, then we have to keep her. If she is not in the witness list then it means the level of threat will be minimal and she has to go back to her normal life," she said.

Family rep was unrelenting. She wanted answers and immediate ones at that. "Are you married?" "Yes." "Do you have children?" "Yes."

"How many?" The handler was not supposed to provide any information about herself. I only knew her by the name she had told me, Suposita. Family rep was asking too many questions. I could feel my handler cornered.

"Don't ask her too many questions," I warned Family rep. We were only supposed to relate at a professional level. But she went mercilessly on and on. I think she was driven by anxiety, the family's anxiety and her concern for my well-being and safety.

"So how do you ensure she is safe? Where is she staying?"

"She is not supposed to tell you," I butted in.

"I would not want to come there anyway, so what is her future?" Family rep asked.

"Well, if she is not a witness then she will have to go back to her old life. We will have to resettle her back into society."

"And how will you know she is not under threat? Will the full witness list ever come from The Hague?" Family rep was indignant.

"Of course, if she is not in the witness list, then whoever was threatening her will lose interest in her," my handler responded.

"Am I in the witness list?" I asked Family rep if she had been in touch with my lawyers.

"Yes, I have been in touch with your lawyers and the ICC says there has been too much fuss over you. They no longer need you as a witness."

"So now that I am not a witness, what next?" I posed.

"So, are you going to abandon her fast like that? This lady has been victimised by the ICC. She is the product of grave injustice. Her future is already destroyed. She definitely cannot go back to her normal life. Are you going to abandon her?"

Family rep was adamant.

The handler kept quiet, seemingly overwhelmed by the probe. I was not sure if Family Rep was directing her questions at the right person. I knew Family rep was right but this luncheon with the handler now sounded like a court room. I shuddered that this could work against me.

"I am not supposed to discuss these issues with you. I was only supposed to drop your Family Rep for your meeting, leave you for about two hours, go back to my office and come back when you are through," my handler said politely.

But Family rep acted as if they had not heard the handler and continued with aggressive cross examination.

"God has a plan for everything. He is the one who planned for this meeting. He knew that we would meet. Nothing happens by coincidence. God chose you to be this lady's handler so you could help her. I am begging you to help this lady. Be human! This girl has no life. She cannot do her normal work. She needs to keep sane. She is someone who had her own job. Now she is tucked away somewhere in a safe house. She cannot reach or contact her family, friends, colleagues or relatives. She cannot even have sex. Surely, she is a social animal," Family Rep was desperate in search for a solution and an end to this.

The handler laughed. Perhaps she was used to this kind of desperation from relatives of clients in witness protection and was desensitised to drama.

"It is true though that I am the only person who is in touch with her! And if you want to meet her you have to go through me," she added.

"And you have to limit your conversation anyway. Our sister has no life. Her life has come to a standstill because of this grave injustice caused to her by Donata. I really feel these people have been unfair to her. After they contacted her and exposed her life to danger, they dare say they no longer need her."

Family rep wanted to cry and I bit my lips and fought back tears welled up in my eyes. I tried to distract my emotions. I cut off a huge chunk of the steak from my plate and filled my mouth with it. I did not feel the taste and I asked Family Rep to pass the salt and chilli sauce.

The issue of my boyfriend had come up in the conversation. "If she has a boyfriend, she has to let us know. Then we have to arrange for him to meet her," my handler said. This seemed to annoy Family Rep who glared at my handler with butcher-knife sharp eyes.

"This lady is very close with her mother. Being unmarried and alone, they are buddies. Now she cannot talk to her mother. Her mother has even refused to answer her phone calls since she was told it was tapped. We had to lie to her that we moved her out of the country. She said that was a better option but she never asks about her anymore."

"Ok, then maybe we can arrange for her mother to be brought over to meet her one of these days," said the handler. "Fact is, she is too old and sickly now and she can't travel," Family Rep said.

How I missed my mother - so loving, understanding, strong and supportive. I recalled how she welcomed me with open arms when I had appeared at home at 5.00 am, despite warnings from those in the protection that the last place I should go to was home. I did it against my better judgment. She was ready to die for me.

She was calm, yet so concerned.

"No Mama, I have little time. I will endanger your life if I stay here longer. I will endanger the life of the whole family." I pleaded.

"You cannot leave. I will hide you in my room. You need not worry. No one will find you here."

But my sister, who was in the next room intervened.

"No, she cannot stay here as much as we would want her to. They will abduct her from here. She has to leave immediately." Mama insisted I must take porridge and sweet potatoes before leaving. I eerily felt as if she was giving me her last blessings. Family organised for a taxi in a few minutes and soon I was on the run again.

My thoughts fell immediately on Wolf, my friend for eight years. He lived in Belgium. I knew he was agonising over this, wondering where I was and if I was still alive. The witness protection document I had signed did not allow me to get in touch with anybody. I did not want to break the trust as this would result in immediate termination of my contract. Wolf, how everything had changed our grand plans. He was to come visit me in the country ahead of our future plans. We were both saving so when he came I would take him round the country – to watch one of the seven wonders of the world, "the wildebeest migration" in the Mara, to Shimba Hills where I had once watched the elephants dance and was almost attacked by a rogue elephant during our nature walk, to the beaches of Mombasa and, of course, home to introduce him to my mother.

The moment I felt I was in danger, I had immediately informed Wolf and he had googled and sent me the mail of the website for the CPJ. That was when I met Karoli, the coordinator. CPJ was founded in 1981 and has its headquarters in New York. It is an independent non-profit organisation dedicated to the global defence of press freedom and takes action whenever journalists are attacked, imprisoned, killed, kidnapped, threatened or censored. They help evacuate journalists from a dangerous zone to a safer location. Karoli liaised with the New York office and asked me to fill some forms, held a meeting with his colleagues to assess the legitimacy of my case. The following day, he advised me to leave my house and go to a friend's place. I packed bare essentials: a pair of trousers, polo neck, one pair of underwear and a toothbrush.

My brother had advised me to go to Narok and stay at a guest house called Siongiroi. The fear of being alone in a place I did not know well or had friends sent my adrenaline reeling in wild thoughts. Wolf had contacted Karoli and they had agreed that I should go to Belgium and stay at Wolf's place until matters cooled down. It was a much better option than going to a refugee camp in a strange country where I knew no one. This was just a temporary situation, or so we thought and everything would go away soon.

By the time the Belgian embassy denied me a visa on account of inability to corroborate my story, Wolf had written an undertaking agreement to care for my medical expenses and provide my accommodation and food. I did not want to be blacklisted, so I maintained my cool despite the rudeness of the Consul at the Embassy. How it hurt me deeply that he did not trust me! How it hurt me deeply that his email implied I had created the story to get myself a visa to Belgium! How it hurt me deeply to know that he believed The Hague instead of me, yet they were the ones telling lies and I was the one telling the truth!

I thanked him and urged Wolf to help ensure my security. Things were tight.

"What do you want?" Family rep asked, after the handler left us alone to catch up on private family issues.

"This is not a life. I have everything I need. I am miserable. I need to mingle with other human beings. I need to walk out in the fresh air without feeling restricted or followed," I said.

"I really appreciate the protection I am getting but please save me. Get me away from here. Take me out of the country or to any other unknown relative, so I can start life afresh. That cannot happen here!" I whimpered.

"What if I got you a job here?" Family Rep asked.

"It would be difficult, if it is the same state agents looking for me. I am not a darling of the system since I exposed corruption and other vices. I have no goodwill from the Government. Anyway, I will survive," I said, with determination.

I reflected on the situation of illegal immigrants all over the world. I had just read the trauma and tribulations of immigrants or those seeking asylum carried in the local dailies and the scenario had depressed me. A local paper ran a feature following the disappearance of some African athletes in the London 2012 Olympics. My handler was getting impatient. We hugged with Family rep and I went back to the house with a heavy heart. But I had hope.

"Give me time. Let us weigh the options, let me think over this whole thing rationally," she said.

I was happy to have met family rep yet I felt mentally exhausted, physically drained like an overworked donkey. All these thoughts about my fate and my future, were working heavily on my mind. Back in the safe house, I made *ugali* and cabbages. The *ugali* did not cook. It tasted soggy. I forced it tastelessly down my throat with some hot chocolate. I lay in bed and tried to embrace sleep but she remained alien to me. I stayed awake for a long while. As I murmured prayers through tears, I wondered if the God of my father and mother was somewhere in the vicinity, listening to the cry of a wretched soul.

"Almighty God, Heavenly Father, I come before your presence this night as helpless as a baby. My sweet Father, I just want to give You thanks and praise, Lord, for always being so good to me. Thank you for the wonderful opportunity You have given me today to meet with family rspective. Thank you, Lord for this beautiful house You have given me and my handlers and all those working with her to take care of me.

"Holy Lord, Mighty Father, King of Kings and Lord of Lords,

I worship you, I glorify You, I magnify your name, I lift you up, King of Glory. What could I do without you my Father? I am just but a poor sinner. Have mercy on me my Lord, I need You so much now. Please open my ways. Bless my plans Oh Lord. You know everything my Father. Your eyes are so wide that You can see the furthest end of the earth. You can reach the highest mountain and the depth of the deepest sea. Lord please reach out to all those who can help me. I know you have great plans for me, Oh my Lord. I love you. I trust You deeply my Protector. Protect me from evil. I know you have great plans for me as you had for Jeremiah. Oh Father, plans for success, for a great future. Give me the grace to forgive Donata even though she has been so bad to me! Thank You Lord, for your promises to me…"

I must have fallen asleep in the middle of my prayer because when I woke up it was dawn. April 2013, as the world waited for the PEV trial to begin, I could not help but marvel at the trail of injustice the ICC had left along her path as it pursued justice. The face of justice was tainted, disfigured, unrecognizable to me.

After the luncheon with Family rep, I felt more abandoned than ever. I could not tell if my handler felt harassed by family representative. I had sent a thank you message to her that night and wished her goodnight but she did not respond.

The following day at 11.30 am, I received a call from her number but the voice was different. A lady said she was calling on behalf of the handler who had forgotten her phone in the office. This was Friday. "You will therefore not hear from her until Monday!" she said. "Okay," was all I said - so much for protection? If the only person I was in touch with had forgotten her phone in the office, then what would happen if I had an emergency? The words of the witness protection officers sounded a familiar bell in my ears. "You are your own best protection. You are your own Best Protection. You are Your own best protection."

I woke up on Saturday morning to heavy head loaded with a sack of more questions than answers. I sought to view the more positive side of life. So far God had been good to me and I had not felt ill at all since the beginning of all this drama. I pinched myself in the ears and arms to confirm if I was still alive.

I picked the newspapers from under the door and looked at the headlines.

Parliament had passed a bill deleting clauses that needed them vetted on integrity issues. I went to the kitchen and vetted the fridge. I was spoilt for choice over what to eat. The fridge was fully stocked (I must give credit to the handlers for giving me enough allowance to live comfortably), only the appetite lacked. There were two crates of eggs, beef and chicken, sausages, chipolatas, pork and beef salamis, tinned beans, liver, *githeri*…I checked the cupboard; cornflakes, Weetabix, marmalade, bread, blue band, honey, sour porridge, pineapple fruit, mango juice, lemon, apples. I stared at the food listlessly but did not touch it.

I warmed a glass of milk in the microwave and added some chocolate, went back to bed, sipped the drink slowly as I read the newspapers. I could not concentrate or understand how this situation played out. I felt my human rights were being violated under this witness protection programme. How could I be in my own country and not be able to see or contact my friends, family, colleagues? How could I not be able to walk freely to wherever I wanted? I wanted to be told how far the investigations had gone. Who had been trailing me and why? Who had tapped my phones? Who had hacked my email? What next?

How long was I going to be indoors in this strange part of the country? I felt treated like a baby. I got very scanty information from my handlers. They assured me it was for my own good.

What a secretive society? What secretive persons! If they were not prepared to give me any information on what they were doing with my life, I decided I would not give them any information either. I asked my handler if I could pull out of the programme since she had told me it was a temporary two-week arrangement. She told me it was not easy to leave now that I was in. No one could walk out of the program just like that! I started thinking of ways to escape out of the country quietly without anyone's knowledge.

When I signed the government witness protection form, I was terrified, traumatised and afraid to die. I was ready to do anything that would help save my life. But now that I was slightly settled, it dawned on me that the moment I signed the forms, I had become government property and I could not do whatever I wanted anymore. It left a bad taste in my mouth.

Now that my handler had forgotten her phone in the office, I had three whole days to myself, without censure. I was tempted to travel to the village and see my mother, sneak into a relative's or friend's place and spend the night. But a voice inside my head warned me. Stop! Think! Self-discipline! Comply with the rules. I listened to my inner voice. After all, it was my life that was in danger and not that of my handler. Patience, I repeated. I curled into bed, covered my head with a blanket and slept the whole day. I slept in most of that Sunday and woke up at about 5.00 pm. I felt hungry. I made dinner as I listened to the BBC news on the death of Neil Armstrong, American astronaut and the first person to walk on the moon. "He was the greatest of all times." Compliments came flowing in.

I watched my favourite Mexican soap opera, *Pasion Morena*, and went to bed, shocked by just how evil people could be.

"Thank You Lord for this new day, I can feel your presence around me my Father. Thank you for protecting me." I whispered the next morning.

I was getting more prayerful and closer to God than I had been in a long time.

I switched on the television, the national conference on Peaceful Elections was going on at Bomas of Kenya. The speeches were long and verbose.

"The law will not wink and justice never sleeps" – Chief Justice Dr. Willy Mutunga said in his speech. I loved that, I loved good quotes and they were rare to come by these days. I switched off the TV and wandered around the house.

I had always been a newspaper addict. But now I was bored with all the time in the world – of my uncertain life. So, I read, read and read. My life was now centred on newspapers and a plug of BBC in my ears even when I was asleep. I knew everything happening in all parts of the world, from the threatening hurricane Sandy in Florida to the sisters of death, selling illicit liquor made of ARVs and formalin in the Korogocho slums of Nairobi.

I switched on the television again. Speech after speech. Oh, how politicians loved speeches, how they loved the sound of their voices! Everybody seemed to wear a black suit today. "The cost of botched elections is extremely high", Prime Minister Raila Odinga recalled, to the amusement of the audience. He narrated how as a presidential candidate he went to vote in Lang'ata, only to find his name missing from the election register. He dashed to the KICC to find the place fortified like a military camp. Finally, his name was found to be in the controversial black book.

President Kibaki's wish was for the children of Kenya to have access to education. This, he said, could only thrive in a peaceful environment. He made fun in his usual off the cuff remarks that elections were only a one-day affair after which people should go back to their normal business. He urged Kenyans to take bribes if they must from candidates but to ensure there was peace during elections, at the end of the day.

Then choirs sang but these lyrics from one of the songs pierced my soul. (Take heart, temptations are like fire that consumes the soul, I pray Lord, help me.)

Some songs touch one's mind so deeply. I felt as if this song was composed for me. My faith had indeed been shaken by this ICC saga. Even as I prayed and persevered, I hoped I could keep sane, that madness would not engulf me.

I switched channels like a couch potato as I whiled away time and gauged my mood. I watched a lioness preying on the wildebeest feeding on the grass, unaware that the lioness was right behind it, hiding in the long savannah grass, scheming, planning for it as its menu for dinner. Nature's hostile plan of checks and balances played out perfectly. I felt like the wildebeest, innocently caught in the web of a criminal court that had destroyed my life, my future, and made me a fugitive in my own country through its scheming. I felt at one with the wildebeest – both of us captured unjustly by the cruel hands of destiny. The only difference between the wildebeest and me was that I was not dead yet. I still had a chance to find a way out of this.

The video clip of battered faces of the Mombasa Republican Army chilled my blood and raised goose pimples all over my body. I felt cold like fresh fish straight from Lake Victoria. I didn't know what exactly had transpired at the scene of arrest but there seemed to be a countdown to justice. What seemed clear was that in the course of justice an injustice was committed. It happened in the battle fields, where women and young girls were raped and taken away as sexual prisoners. It happened when young boys were forced to become child-soldiers. It happened during police raids when the men in uniform stole jewellery, money and other valuables in the course of pursuing justice. It had happened in hospitals, where directors who tried to save lives ended up in prison docks for denying women a chance to give birth.

Injustice had happened to me too. Donata, while pursuing justice for PEV, had endangered my life and turned me into a fugitive, held me away from a bright future, like a snake in a dark bottomless pit latrine, like a fish out of water.

Many policemen were injured while fighting justice in Coast region – in the Tana River, Witu, Kengeleni, among others. I knew those areas well because I had covered politicians during the 2007 election campaigns. Our crew almost had a fatal accident when a rogue hippo jumped out of the Tana River at Witu. Our skilled driver missed it by a whisker. It was about 8.00 pm and we rushed to an area where we could find communication network to file our stories on phone. Journalists in the field were always a pulse away from death. We were permanently on the road, driving through dangerous spots and bandit prone roads of Mpeketoni, Witu through to Lamu.

Yet we never thought of death. We thought of the story and how we would be the first to break the news. Even if we did not get involved in accidents, we faced hostile crowds who at times broke our cameras, tore our notes and battered us up. Crowds who felt we had committed an injustice by exposing their private lives or abused their favourite politicians.

Journalists like Mo Amin and Hos Maina had died in the line of duty. I listened keenly on Mashujaa Day to hear the names of these two but no! As one politician had once said, "journalists were born by the roadside." It is ironic that when the public wanted to use us, they would look for us everywhere to report the loss of their abducted children or kidnapped family members, politicians would call us for their rallies only to later turn their backs on us, having used us like tissue paper.

For many journalists there is always a countdown to justice. It is called the curse of being a journalist.

CHAPTER ELEVEN

Lemon or Lemonade

DONATA PULLED A CHAPTER OUT OF MY LIFE like a dentist at work and replaced it with artificial dentures. The life I lived now was no longer mine. It was fear-driven.

I still nursed a toothache several weeks after the filling had fallen off. The pain was getting unbearable. As I soothed the gap with my tongue, I knew the time had come for me to see the dentist. I had repeatedly shelved the visit, but now I had no choice.

After I failed to sleep the previous night, I had to be sensible and face the dentist's knife. I thought of the long syringe that would go painfully into my mouth, of the sharp pain I would feel before the anaesthesia settled. And then the pluck, pluck! I closed my eyes. I trembled. Pain, pain go away, please come back another day. The pain hung around, dull. I knew at night it would wake up and take away my sleep. Silly toothache, it did not even see that I had enough problems of my own. It should have waited until I was ready.

At 10.30 pm as I went to sleep, I had not heard from my handler. I had sent her two messages but there was no reply. This was the fifth straight day that I had not heard from her.

I knew she had abandoned me. Perhaps she was offended by Family Rep's questions. I knew I was on my own. I switched off the phone. "God, I am alone. Please hold my hand. Please take control. Please be that close friend to me that sticks closer than a brother. Thank you, Lord. I am safe in your arms. I am safe under your wings Lord. I took the medicine, switched off the lights and went to sleep. *"Kesho pia ni siku,"* (tomorrow is another day) I said.

When I woke up in the morning, I felt better, tried to be kind to myself. I tried sleep but my eyes refused to close. I stared at the white ceiling for a while and saw shadows that looked like Donata playing on the roof. I jumped out of bed and emptied the dustbin. The dustbin van came only once a week (on Wednesday) and if I missed it, I would have to keep two weeks of rubbish.

I brushed my teeth reluctantly only to realise I had broken some of the post dental recovery rules. In an effort to finish everything quickly and rush, I gurgled cold water without salt and brushed the tooth next to the socket against the commandments. I quickly ate a cold banana and drank a glass of water, took the painkiller and went back to bed. I was disappointed that sleep had vanished. A song we had once sang at the school assembly kept ringing in my head. If I sang out loudly as I often did, I would distract my mouth. I hummed the words quietly, my eyes closed.

As far as I was concerned, a toothache was one of the world's terrible trials. I got up and dialled my handler's number but she did not pick up the phone. A minute later, she called back.

"I forgot my phone in one of our offices and it's out of the way – was also busy trying to sort out issues. I got back my phone yesterday and I was going to call you today," she said. I missed home. I missed my mother, my wonderful nieces and nephew too. I wondered how my Mama had managed to go through the old cultural practices of my community of having her six lower teeth removed.

My Mama often told me that sad story of how at 11, she was kidnapped by her neighbours on her way to school. They removed her six lower teeth using a short spear and forced her to bite on hot *ugali* to stop the bleeding. "It was the most painful thing in my life," she said.

Perhaps that is what had contributed to my phobia of dentists and my profuse sweating and trembling whenever I passed by a dentist's clinic. My Mama and her generation were so brave to have gone through this rite. I was glad the community had discarded it completely and although many people were going back to their traditions of facing the knife, my community had steered clear of the practice and many who had gone through the tradition had replaced their teeth with artificial dentures.

My gum healed slowly. Five days later, it was still sore. I longed for a cold red devil ice cream but memories of the dentist's clinic made me drop the thought instantly. I was determined to avoid anything that would take me back to the knife.

Meanwhile, Donata's knife continued piercing sharply.

CHAPTER TWELVE

No Time to Die

I WAS NOT SURE THAT I WAS PREPARED TO DIE. That is why I was in hiding, afraid of the people who trailed me, afraid of the people who wanted to hurt me, those who believed that I was a witness at The Hague.

What had I done to the gods that they should set their wrath on me? Whose funeral had I failed to attend? Had I talked ill of the dead? Why, why was death following me on the wings of The Hague?

I had not prepared well for my death. I had lived as if I was here on earth forever. I was busy making future arrangements with Wolf, not aware that fate would separate us for a very long time, perhaps forever!

I did not have much property but I should have put my act together – written my will. I had discussed my fears with the psychoanalyst when I was taken for assessment at a Nairobi Hospital, a procedure at the witness protection program. I was traumatised and very afraid. Afraid that someone might shoot me from the back as I walked on the streets. I feared someone might fire 18 bullets through my body, as had happened to people considered enemies of the state.

My two best friends prayed but still died terrible, painful deaths from cancer. I would let God worry on my behalf. As the elders said, nobody knew what kind of death one would suffer - whether it would be an illness, a road accident, a bullet or an air crash. Only God knows. He has plans for everyone's D-day. One only has to be ready. The day and time are His, still this did not stop me from running away. They say God helps those who help themselves. I was helping myself by hiding from my pursuers and God would help me. That I believed.

I was annoyed with God. This Hague business instilled doubt in my mind. For the first time, I toyed with questions around God's existence and why He had picked on me. Then I bargained with him and tried to blackmail Him. If He truly loved me, He should have let me get on with my life and not make me so miserable… Then I made Him promises, some of which I knew I could not keep. I did not know if God was happy or angry with me.

Now that I was in trouble, facing death any time, I had resorted to prayer. I prayed a lot, asking God to forgive me for abandoning Him, for feeling self-righteous, for failing to show up in church during Christmas and New Year festivities.

I sang a lot. I hoped, I believed God had forgiven me. I believed he had put me through this test to draw me back to Him.

As days went by, I made a deliberate effort to forgive all those who had sinned against me. The list was long but as I remembered them, I forgave them, hoping that God would forgive me too. "I love you my Lord," I would say several times a day blowing kisses towards Heaven.

It was a wonder that I could remember the words of most hymns. I sang in church before I got to the age of ten. Those hymns strengthened me.

Now and then I asked my guardian angels to protect me

against danger and the curse of The Hague.

These spiritual trophies like hymns and prayer are what I relied on as I waited for my uncertain future. And as I prayed, I joined Jeremiah 29:11 in hope. "For I know the plans I have for you, says the Lord. Plans to prosper you and not to harm you, plans to give you hope and a future". The future was in His hands. Human justice had failed. I now waited patiently for God's justice.

For the one week I had not heard from my handlers, it took self-discipline and a desire to stay alive not to hunt down my relatives or friends. At my last meeting with family representative, in the presence of the handlers, she brought me dozens of storybooks. These kept me busy. The man who brought me newspapers daily had travelled upcountry and would be away for a while. I got up earlier and listened to the newspaper reviews on TV. It was not the same but at least I was roughly in touch with the day's events. A song crossed my mind – Freedom. Being a strong member and lead vocalist of our high school choir, we rehearsed the song Freedom taught to us by our choir master, Mr. Auma. We really did not know the true meaning of the lyrics but we liked the vocals.

"Freedom…oh…freedom
Compelling the power to all mankind
The underprivileged and OAU states
Shall join their forces and fight all
Forms of suppression"

That was one of the best times in my life. We rode in the school bus to the District, Provincial and then National Music festivals to the city, 400 km away. Lunch was a half-loaf bread and a bottle of Fanta for everyone. Bread tasted sweet – sweeter than sugar and honey. The rich girls bought chicken and chips. Some of us were survivors. We really did not care. Back home, chicken was served at Christmas or some other special ceremony, like dowry payment ceremonies. We ignored those excesses and enjoyed the bread.

My handlers informed me one morning that I was not in the list of witnesses at The Hague. I felt a sense of relief after the long wait. They suggested that I re-join the community in order to lead a normal life, once again.

"What about my security?" I queried. "The indictees will be too busy working on their defence that they will not have time to think about you!" they advised. I was not convinced by my handlers' intentions to release me back to the streets. They had no information on who my trailers were and could not vouch for my safety once I was back in my house. I promised myself that I would not walk out of the safe house into the mouth of lions on the prey, seeking out perceived or real Hague witnesses or do a repeat of running for my life. I started planning carefully on how to get out of the country.

Kind friends, strangers and relatives helped me apply for a visa and paid for my air ticket. An honest Mama Mboga, selling onions, kales and avocado outside the safe house, successfully delivered my note to a friend, who mobilised people I trusted into the scheme. They wrote letters, emails, made calls while all I did was pray on my knees.

Where there is a will there is a way. Whenever one path was blocked, God opened another. I trusted in God and started packing even before I was called for the visa interview. When God had worked his miracle and I had it safely in my hands, I asked the Witness Protection Agency to release me so I could travel to a safer destination.

My handlers handed me over to a trusted friend and relative who drove me to the Jomo Kenyatta International Airport and ensured I boarded the flight through Qatar to the US without any hitches. They alerted me that I am still a potential witness as they were still investigating who had been following me in unmarked cars and on foot. They asked me to get in touch with them as soon as I arrived at my destination, which I did.

They told me that since I had opted out of the Witness Protection voluntarily, they would not cater for my needs or give me any compensation according to the rules and regulations. I felt sad as I bid my four handlers goodbye. They had become part of my family, the only people I had been with for the most part of this journey. As we parted, I had this forlorn feeling that I would not see them again.

As I boarded the plane at the airport, a sad feeling overwhelmed me and I felt hot salty tears sting my eyes and then trickle down my face. I wondered if I would ever see my beloved Mama, family, friends and colleagues again.

EPILOGUE

Memories of an African Christian childhood

One year in the safe house was almost like ten years to me. Yet a lot of times, instead of focusing on the future, my childhood memories flooded my mind. Nostalgic memories of those days of innocence flooded my thoughts and brought both laughter and tears to my eyes.

Then we did not know the word tribe and some of my classmates were my best friends. It is only years later when I grew up that I learnt that they were from a different tribe and we could no longer sit at the same table or drink from the same cup. In the same way that Jesus had opened the eyes of the blind man at the pool of Bethsaida after years of protection from this world, did my eye open to the truth of Kenyan tribal politics. I learnt of their people and my people, their God and our god, their language and our language. I learnt derogatory words like *okuyo mwizi jarabuon* (Kikuyu thief, potato lover) and *jaluo kihii* (uncircumcised Luo). My vocabulary expanded with my years.

We were cheeky children but we loved the Lord. We respected both church and culture. We loved to sing, dance and to go to Sunday school, read and play. We prayed first thing in the morning, during meals, after dinner and before bed. We climbed on trees to pick ripe mangoes, guavas and fat worms. Monkeys often chased us away but we were not deterred. Together with other children, mostly siblings, neighbors or school-mates, we stole little stuff from the kitchen – sugar, cooking oil, salt, vegetables and hot charcoal.

Sometimes our elders caught us with our hands in the honey jar. We got a smack here, a punishment there, a prayer here, a warning there but all this did not deter us from yielding to temptation again and again.

We played *kalongolongo* – the children's cookery game. We imitated our mama's cooking, scooped mud after a rainy day and sculptured tables, seats, plates and spoons. We made muddy meals and prayed to God to bless our *kalongolongo* meal before we served ourselves. Our menu was enticing; mud cake, mud corn bread, mud fish, mud potatoes and mud stew.

At an early age when we could have died of cholera, bilharzia, amoeba, pneumonia, malaria or provided shelter for earthworms, tapeworms, jiggers and other diseases, God protected us and so did our ancestral spirits. Many a child in our village of Kondele, Kisumu Town on the shores of Lake Victoria did not make it to the age of five years. Many did not have the privilege of being born in hospital or vaccinations. God was gracious to us. Our parents kept us away from watching the burials of other children. The elders said this would bring us bad luck and we would quickly follow the departed ones to the grave.

It was the age of innocence. We exploited every single opportunity to play, which was our priority, from dawn to dusk. When the rains came accompanied by thunder and lightning, we took advantage of the first few drops. We poked our tongues with frenzy and with cherish savored the drizzles from the sky as we chanted, *"koth chwe to chieng' rieny ondiek onywol ei aora"* (It's raining and shining concurrently, a hyena has had a baby in the river.)

As children, we learnt from our elders that the rains were both a blessing and God's own tears and thunder was God's angry roar at our sins. So, when thunder struck, we bolted under our beds. When God was super angry, he struck a tree or a sinful person. The dead person was said to have worn a red attire . I learnt early in my childhood that God did not like people who wore red clothes when it was raining. Red was a color associated with evil spirits. Red was associated with mourning and death. People who wore red were perceived to be witches ready to cause havoc in the community. When Mama and Baba took us Christmas shopping once a year, I would beg them not to buy me a red dress. I did not want to be struck by lightning.

Raindrops were cold, fresh and sweet. Little did we know the dangers of drenching wet and catching pneumonia, a cough and other infections. Well, we children wanted to fall sick, anyway.

It was a privilege to be admitted at Russia Provincial Hospital, The General Hospital, Lake Nursing Home or Ka-Shabir. This was the only time visitors brought patients soda, queen cakes from the popular local Mayfair Bakeries, fresh or sour Mala milk – all a luxury. This was that once in a blue moon that one took advantage of one's illness and asked for fried eggs any time of the day or night.

Ka-Shabir Hospital stood opposite the Kenyatta Sports Ground. It was arguably the most popular hospital in town. Doctor Shabir did not ask patients for a deposit fee before treatment as they do in hospitals today. He did not detain a patient in the wards nor made them peel potatoes and scrub toilet floors when they could not raise the bill. He let people go.

If you promised to pay later and failed to do so, he let it rest. That was between you and your God, he said. He said he had done his bit as a doctor. It was up to you to do your bit. Most patients paid later. But he never followed anyone who failed to pay later. However, the God of Shabir was said to be powerful. When Shabir called on Him, the debtor would be seen at the animal market selling a goat or a chicken and headed with the money straight to the hospital's billing office.

I remember Mama's gentle and worried voice as she asked me with concern, "You have not eaten anything, child. Sorry you feel so ill. What does your heart tell you? What does it want?"

"Oh Mama, I don't want to eat anything. I have no appetite!" I responded weakly, although deep down in my heart, I really wanted to ask for my favorite dish.

"Can you taste a bit of fried eggs, just a tiny *winy* little spoonful?' Mama goaded.

"Yes Mama, I can try," I whispered, quite pleased at the suggestion and pretended not to be interested. I wasn't all that ill anyway. I had only hurt my right toe in a silly accident.

As a little six-aged girl , I was quite adventurous. When we visited our grandparents in the village, we used a pit latrine. The pit latrine was scary. If you peeped inside, you could see a deep bottomless pit. It was dizzying just trying to figure out how deep the hole went. Often, we pretended to go inside the toilet but when no one was watching, we would run and do "it" behind the toilet. We then ran off as fast as our naughty legs could run.

Katolo was my heaven and *kora* my dancing cloud. *Katolo* is a game of pebbles. We drew eight square blocks with charcoal, stepped on one foot and skillfully kicked pebbles round all the blocks without touching the edges. In *kora*, we sat cross-legged on the ground, collected neat round pebbles, about 10, threw one in the air, collected the nine before the one in the air came tumbling down your palm. Pebbles were important to children then, like coins. On the way home from school, I would take my time sampling pebbles. I hid them in a corner in my school bag among the books, the rounder the better.

On a bright sunny morning, we jumped after the big grasshoppers in the long green grass. We loved the little green nymphs *(dede)* because they were just babies. They could not jump as fast as their mothers and we caught them easily. You simply cupped your hands over their shadows and that was done. We dipped them in bottles and fed them with grass and water. A few died and we felt sad and released the others back to their mothers. Then we would hold a decent burial for the dead nymphs, really wishing their parents could attend. We knew every living thing had a father and mother.

When babies died, mothers sang funeral dirges. They invoked the greedy gods of the earth who were so fast that they swallowed their kids in the bellies of the grave before their time. We sang the same dirges for the nymphs as we dug shallow graves with sticks to send them off. Then we sang the funeral hymns. When someone died in the village, the elders first wailed and danced around the compound and sang funeral dirges.

Then the church men came, led by the priest, and the dirges stopped. Everyone composed themselves and joined in the hymns. The church men said to cry for the dead was a sin. They opened the holy Book and read that part that said one who cried was lost and had no hope in the resurrection of the body. Our elders said that the children had gone to Heaven. We did not question them. Children were supposed to be seen and not heard. But we children knew the little secret that the bodies were in the soil behind the house in the banana plantation.

It was rare to catch the big grasshoppers. They tricked us when they changed their color from green to brown. So, to catch one was a big feat. We begged our aunts to give us a piece of hot charcoal to roast our catch. The insects were delicious. The aunts loved them too. When they did not give us hot charcoal, they roasted them for us but ate most of the portion.

My favorite game was *Awuor* followed by climbing mango trees. On a dry day, some black insect that looked like a beetle (locally known as *Awuor Awuor)* made holes in the ground. It was easy to identify Awuor's hole. It was different from a lot of other insects. She covered her hole with a mound and raised her swollen dusty back above the ground. She understood human language. She understood our local dialect Dholuo. When children sang to her and urged her to show herself, she obediently shook the ground and came out.

Awuor got her name from a local folktale. She was a beautiful insect woman with her nose up in the air. She had many suitors from the animal world. They sought her hand in marriage; hyenas, birds, tortoises, snakes, monkeys, hare. She turned them down one after the other. Her younger sister often went to the farm where Awuor Awuor was busy weeding her crops. She sang to alert her of the presence of a suitor at home.

"Awuor pack up your bags and come home. You have a guest!" Her sister called.

"Who is it this time? What does he look like?" She inquired.

"The guest is a Hawk – he who steals chicken!" Her sister responded.

"Please tell him to go away!" Awuor Awuor said and went back to work.

She finally married a weaver bird.

When I tapped the ground gently with the palm of my hands and sang softly, Awuor Awuor came out of her hole. This filled my heart with joy. It meant Awuor Awuor had found a husband. I pretended to be a male suitor. I celebrated, danced around the hole and went back to the house, happy that there was a wedding in the animal world. Of course, I knew which animal Awuor Awuor had chosen as her groom. She only came out of her hole if she liked the animal I named in the song.

As children, we paid great attention to insects, especially ants. When the older members of the family shared Bible Study after dinner, they talked about a great man called Solomon who was full of wisdom. The ants had one day invited Solomon to their kingdom and he was astonished at how developed and civilized the ant kingdom was.

Other animals were not as gracious as Awuor. The *senesene* were secretive and often rebellious. They were brown and had white fluffy wings. They came out mostly in the evening when we got ready for bed. They flew out of their holes in their thousands, like a world war army and hurried straight to the street lights or any lamp posts. But they could not survive the light for long. Like moths, once they were blinded, they lost their will and wings and fell helplessly in piles on the ground. They left the anthills with permission from their queen mother, whom we were told stayed put in the deepest corner, fiercely guarded by several harsh *senesene* soldiers.

Senesene were stubborn. If you tapped the hole near the mouth of the anthill, they refused to come out. They were a rare delicacy. They planned their exit from the ant-hill in style, waiting a day or two after the rains. The season was coming and we ate Tsenetsene in plenty. We thanked the Lord God of Heaven and Earth for opening the earth's belly and sending us manna from heaven.

The ants marched out of their hole majestically like soldiers at a parade, so delicious, so fatty in their bottoms like the plump women who fetched water from River Oroba, delicately balancing the pots on their heads.

The queen ant was said to be a rare delicacy too. I did not know how she tasted. Culture defined that only men could eat it. Women roasted her and served her whole to men and boys but would not taste it.

There were two giant mango trees inside our compound. My greatest joy was when the mangoes were raw and green. I ran away from Lake Primary School and climbed the trees in my blue school tunic, my green school bag slung across my chest. As I ate the mangoes, I filled my bag with some too. I looked forward to my favorite lunch break song.

"Nasikia Sauti, Nasikia Sauti, Sauti ya Mama.
Sasa ni Saa Sita, Mwalimu kwaheri." (I hear my
mum's voice calling, it's now lunchtime, bye teacher!)

Often, an accident happened – like the sting of a bee or constipation. There was first aid to pull out the bee-sting now swollen with pain, and then a little smack there. But the most sting of them all was that of the wasp – with its tiny waist.

No matter how many times Mama warned us not to climb the trees, we broke the rules – lured by the green mangoes, so enticing, so inviting. But Mama sorted us out by deworming us. It was a terrifying experience that resulted in round and tapeworms evacuating our tummies. This kept us away from the mangoes and guava tress, but only temporarily.

The age of innocence was with us and we forgot the dangers around us. Mama said the God of Elijah, Enoch, Moses, Shadrack, Abednego, Paul, Silas and Jacob protected us when she was not watching over us. She said the God of Shadrack, Meshach and Abednego was so powerful that He had let them walk through fire and they were not scathed. She said the God of Paul and Silas had opened for them the prison doors when they sang for Him. The prison guards' limbs got as soft as the slimy *osuga* vegetables we often had for dinner. They got too helpless and powerless to stop them. Mama sang of a heavenly chariot of horse and fire that plucked Elijah like the Hawk that stole chickens and hushed him in a whirlwind up to Heaven.

Despite being so young and playful, Mama still allocated us duties.

After school, we ground maize-meal at the posho mill in Kondele. It was the only posho mill and was located at the Kibos/Kakamega junction on the way to Nyawita. Posho-mill errands were exciting because it was one of those rare times you got to hold pennies in your hands.

Usually, when I got to the posho mill with a little sack on my head full of maize or sorghum and millet, there was a long queue.

If the posho mill attendant was in a good mood, he would only charge me Ksh2.00. If Mama gave me Ksh2.50, I used the surplus 50 cents to buy sugarcane, jiggery *(sukari nguru)* or groundnuts. It was better deal to carry maize grains to the posho mill because people did not like it when you mixed your sorghum with their white maize.

When the queue was too long, I pleaded with someone with a friendly face in the queue to watch over our sacks a ten-cent fee. Together with other naughty children, we strayed towards Nyawita, where we had discovered a deep secret, a secret from which Christian children and in general the Christian Community was protected – the Busaa Club.

Curiosity got the better of us and we still went and feasted our hungry eyes on men and women dancing to traditional music (the Nyatiti or Lyre).

They were drunk, very drunk from the *busaa* – traditional brew made from millet. The men were fully dressed but the women wore scanty clothes that left their chests bare. They shook their shoulders wildly as if possessed by spirits and sang drunkenly. If it was midday, the scorching Kisumu sun made sweat pour down the body like heavy rains.

A man sang in praise of his lover. Men and women held each

other very tightly. They shook their shoulders vigorously as if possessed by the Holy Spirit on a Pentecostal church day. When the dance got too wild, we ran away and closed our eyes tightly. We picked our flour and chewed sugarcane on our way back as we carefully balanced the baskets on our heads.

"You took rather long today," Mama commented when we got back. "The queue was long Mama," I explained. She was not fooled. Kondele was a small place. A neighbor had seen us heading toward the Busaa Club and followed us there. Baba and Mama already knew what I was up to. That evening, the Bible lesson after dinner was obedience to one's parents.

"Honor your father and mother, that your days may be long in the land the Lord your God has given you." It was from the Ten Commandments from Genesis – Old Testament. I was afraid, really afraid.

I did not want to die. I wanted to live long enough to finish my education and get a good job. I longed to become a good teacher like Joy Mayor who headed the Union School or a missionary like Miss Pam Wilding who taught the ladies secretarial duties at the Church. Maybe I could become a philanthropist like Aunt Sophia Odero. I could learn to play the organ every Sunday in Church like Mama Violet Odero or write books like Asenath Odaga at Thu Tinda Bokshop. I did not go back to the Busaa Club again.

I asked Baba and Mama if I could join the Church choir instead of whiling away at the Busaa Club. They agreed, albeit reluctantly. Mama warned me though, "Child, not everyone in the Church choir is a Christian in character. Singing in church is a ministry. It is a way to spread the gospel. People have different motives for going to church. Be very careful lest the devil leads you into temptation."

We had won the Churches Provincial Music Festival in Kisumu and were headed to Nairobi City, the capital of Kenya for the national competition. It was a ten-hour drive those days. The police arrested our bus in Naivasha, about two hours away from our destination. We had been drinking soda, water and munching bread on the way as we sang different popular Christian tunes. Apparently, some of our members mixed their soda with whisky and got terribly drunk. They no longer sang the gospel songs we had initially sang along the way. They now sang 'dirty' songs – songs of the flesh, songs of the Busaa Club, songs that did not belong in the Church or fit in with the long purple gowns we wore - the color of The Resurrection.

They flipped deeply respected spiritual songs to suit their drunken voices and smartly replaced the lyrics with others, with sexual connotations. Their beautiful angelic voices slurred. They sang like babies learning to talk.

When the police stopped our loaded church bus to do a spot check, they ordered us out of the bus. We waited outside as they got inside the bus and inspected our bags. Naivasha was chilly and the thick fog and mist blurred our vision. A thorough search on some of the luggage revealed drugs – hard drugs, and a sea of whisky. Some of the bottles were full, others half empty. The devil in the bottle blurred the vision of some of our choir members.

We never got to Nairobi for the competition. After a cold night in the bus at the police station, we travelled back to Kisumu – by order of the Church Committee. We were the shame of the church, the face of the devil. I was only 11 and was hardly aware of what was going on inside the bus. I had slept most of the way. I dreamt of the big hall in the city, crowded with thousands of fans cheering us wildly as we picked the winning trophy. All I remembered was that the bus felt slimy after some of our drunken mates threw up all over the bus. I thought it was something they ate.

When we reached Kisumu, the Bishop informed us that

the choir was dissolved. Some members were expelled from the Church, others expelled like Jonah from the mouth of the whale. Baba and Mama kept me away from the choir even after it was constituted a year later. It hit me with a cold bang that Church was not the heaven I thought it was.

Hidden Agenda

THERE WERE PEOPLE WITH HIDDEN AGENDA. As choir members, we lost our reputation. We abused the opportunity we had to spread the gospel of Christ through songs. That is what happened when you made friends with the devil – he would shame you, expose you to everybody, then laugh at you. He would come for your soul at midnight. I was innocent in the bus incident, as some members. But we could not prove it.

Injustice was everywhere. One could not run away from it. Nobody listened to us. We were all responsible for the sins of the choir – it was called collective responsibility. Some choir members who were not expelled departed from the church on their own volition. "A sinner runs away even if no one is after him," church elders told us. Some of us trudged on. We asked God for forgiveness. The Christian journey was not an easy one. Even in church, the water pot had broken.

Yes, we were all sinners. We had fallen short of the glory of God. But he was kind and merciful and would forgive us our sins if only we asked Him. These memories of my childhood reminded me that no one was perfect. The congregation blamed us although not all involved in the trip tasted drugs or alcohol. We dutifully carried the cross on behalf of our brothers and sisters. Mama was philosophical. She said in life's journey, some things just happened out of the blues and took a life of its own. No one had control over it except God. "Father, hear the prayer we offer, not for ease but for strength that we may live our lives courageously," she prayed.

We lost our voices on stage

There was something about me and choirs that did not work out and I began to doubt if choir was really meant for me.

I had fond memories of my old School, Lake Primary School and sad ones too. If I thought the expulsion of members from the church choir was a tragedy, then the events at the school choir may only be termed a disaster. With the church choir dissolved, I asked Baba and Mama if I could join the school choir and they agreed. They, however, repeated the same warning, "Be careful, my daughter," Mama said. "Learn from your past. Do what has taken you to the choir- to sing. Not everyone is there to sing. Some have a hidden agenda.

The Nyanza Schools Music Festival was at the Kisumu Social Center Hall. Hundreds of choirs from different schools across the region arrived on foot, bicycles, buses, and pick-ups. We braced for fierce competition. We eavesdropped on other choirs doing their rehearsals and hoped to steal the show. When we got to the stage in our well-ironed, neat uniforms, we lost voices.

Perhaps it was stage fright. But when we opened our mouths to sing, no sound came out. Not from all the 40 of us. The frustrated choirmaster asked the adjudicators for permission to start again. By then the crowd went loud with laughter and jeers. We completely lost our self-esteem. I quickly called on the Lord to instantly return our voices from wherever the devil had hidden them.

The choirmaster tried again but we had all lost our voices – gone with the wind. We left the stage crying, our self-esteem smashed to smithereens. When all choirs had sung and the results called, we were nowhere in the list. The adjudicators, adding salt to injury called us out as the worst choir in the history of the music festival. We walked with our tails between our legs. We were the ridicule of our schoolmates, especially those who had been denied the privilege of joining the school choir by their lack of talent.

The devil appears in mysterious ways. This was not just a personal shame. It went further. We had shamed our school and made it the laughing stock of the choir fraternity. It was a story of failure, of panic and lack of confidence. It was unfortunate that we never got to sing, considering the long hours of preparation and rehearsals involved. What had gone wrong? We could not tell. We do not know. Our choir mate Connie, more conversant with traditional beliefs insisted that someone in the crowd had bewitched us, out of jealousy.

"Is it the devil Mama?" I asked her. Mama consoled me after she saw my crest-fallen face. Bad news travels fast, like the telegraphs the postman brought when he had the news of death of a loved one. She had already received the news, which was now the talk of town. There was a lovely restaurant in Kisumu next to the Akamba Bus station toward the Kenya Railways station called TOT. TOT was an acronym for Talk of Town and had the best *samosas* and fresh passion juice. TOT was famous for positive reasons. Our choir disaster was TOT for all the wrong reasons. "No daughter it's not the devil. People sometimes accuse the devil of things he has not even done!" Mama said. "It's not the end of the world! Cheer up! These are small things. You are young. Bigger things are still coming ahead. Save your strength for that," she said.

"Nothing is permanent," Baba encouraged me. He chuckled,

amused by the incident but trying not to laugh. Baba had a good sense of humor and always made the best of a bad situation. He had taught us to laugh at our weaknesses so that we could grow stronger and no one would put us down. "People will mock you, have a good laugh and talk about it for a while but it will pass. They will soon forget about it. Something more interesting to talk about will come up," he said. "Baba, why is it that every choir I sing in has a tragic end? Am I cursed?" Baba shook his head. "No," he said. "I know the Lord will make a way for you!"

To support me, my family gathered in the living room after dinner and we all sang the set piece. I felt better. I was grateful to my family for always being there for me. I was reluctant to go to school the following morning but I had no choice. Life had to go on despite its misfortune. There was no room for the weak, for cowards. You did not solve your problems by burying your head in the sand, like the proverbial ostrich.

Only those who had the courage and good sense to face their problems survived - that's what Mama said every day. Problems seemed to surround me as a child. Baba and Mama picked me from school the following day to go and buy new shoes. My shoes were worn out. I had worn them for long and as I grew older and taller, I out-grew them. Otieno, the famous Kondele cobbler had sewn them repeatedly and tried to expand them as much as he could, in vain.

It did not help matters as I stepped on the edges to make them even older. I really longed for new shoes and this was a god send. So, over lunch hour, Mama and Baba drove me in the green family Volkswagen to Bata Shoe Shop in the heart of the town. After we bought the shoes and a pair of white socks, we passed by TOT restaurant and had some finger licking *samosas* and passion juice. My parents then dropped me in school just in time for the afternoon lessons.

Every evening after school, we played 'around us' with plastic balls and bladder. I removed my new shoes and played barefoot, comfortably. When the game was over and it was getting dark, I ran home. Halfway through, I realized that I did not have my new shoes on. I had forgotten them under the tree where we were playing.

Baba and Mama were livid. They could not understand how I lost my new shoes so easily. That evening after dinner, I got a thorough beating. Baba said I deserved it. I was too ashamed to ask God to return my shoes. We never found the shoes. Someone must have helped themselves to them. No amount of plea or threats from the School headmaster, Mr. Owino, would make the thief confess. The teachers went through every pair of shoes in the assembly the following morning but no new shoes were seen. I was very sad. I went back to my old uncomfortable shoes - guiltily. No one talked about new shoes anymore. I learned to live with my circumstances. I was paying the price for too much playing.

In Class 6, my Science teacher, Mr. Obo had intense dislike for me, for reasons I did not know. He started every lesson by knocking my head with the hard back of the Blackboard duster, before he even greeted the class. He then asked me to sit on the cold hard cement floor under the teacher's table for the rest of the lesson. He ordered me to hold my ears.

The position was uncomfortable and it also meant I could not make any notes. I began to hate Science class with a passion. Mr. Obo got on my nerves. Whenever the bell rang for the science class, I trembled in fear.

I mentioned what was happening to Mama. She said I was exaggerating. So, I decided to take matters into my own hands. We did not keep long hair then. It was part of the rules for both male and female pupils to have clean, razor-shaven heads. That's what made Mr. Obo's head-knocks so painful.

The science class came one morning and Mr. Obo knocked my head with his dusty duster as usual, and then sent me under the table. As I sat there, my rage boiled. I watched him with such intense dislike that I could feel the energy ooze from every ounce of my body. He turned his back and wrote some notes on the blackboard. I took my chance. I sneaked on him from the back, jumped on his back, held his ear lobes and hang onto them as if to life itself. I screamed and wailed as if I was the one being attacked.

The teacher screamed in surprise and pain and I screamed back. The children screamed too and jumped out of their seats. "You will never hit me with a blackboard duster again, sir! You will never, ever touch this bald head of mine again, Sir. Over my dead body!" I repeated the words "over my dead body" again and again. The children repeated rhythmically, "Omwa is beating the teacher; Omwa is beating the teacher, wolololololo!"

The class prefect, Meshack, ran to the staffroom to call Mr. Owino. The class monitor, Akinyi, ran down the stairs to Class Three to call Mama. Mama was a teacher at the same school I attended. She taught Classes One to Three. Mr. Owino tried to pull me away from Mr. Obo but I wouldn't budge. It was only when Mama came that I let go of Mr. Obo's ears. It was a great shame, Mama said, what I had done. The teacher's child was supposed to be a role model. What would Baba say? What would God think? I thought I would be expelled from school. Mama was very sad. I had embarrassed her. She asked me to pray and ask God to give me the grace to forgive Mr. Obo.

The other children defended me. I got away with it. I hated Mr. Obo and science throughout school. Mama never said a word or referred to the incident again. I knew she was upset. But as in other past incidents, she struck to her Mantra – that if something was very bad, the best thing was not to talk about it! Instead, she opted to talk to God.

The teacher continued with the science class but he never beat me again. I did poorly in Science in the National Exam and lost the chance to join a national secondary school.

In
Exile

WITH THE 2013 KENYAN ELECTIONS coming up, I got even more frightened that the powerful forces would now be in full control and I would become minced meat, ready to be gobbled by a hungry grave that rejected no one, not even a leper. I quietly made plans and fled the country. I went into exile.

I landed at the Dulles International Airport in Washington on February 15, 2013.

The National Alliance and the United Republican Party alliance, dubbed the Jubilee Coalition, won the elections. Mr. Uhuru Kenyatta became president and Mr. William Ruto his deputy.

I fled into exile into a cold country whose harsh winters burnt my lips and whose hot summers baked my skin and sucked my blood like the Shetani lava of Tsavo West, Taita Taveta that went mad 400 years ago. I longed for the fresh natural waters of the Mzima Springs, waters that could cool my thirst and revitalise my life. High temperatures threatened to turn me into ashes in a country whose culture shock turned my whole life upside down.

It is cold winter in the United States. I monitor The Hague trials with bated breath and I pursue my asylum. The process is tedious and weary. I miss home deeply. Would I ever rise from the ashes? But I have met with kind souls everywhere, souls that have made my life easier to bear and made me a part of the human family once more.

Wolf and I reconnected after I got to America and broke up after we lost contact. I learnt of his death from a heart attack through an inbox message on Facebook three years later. I miss home, but I must say home is where your heart is.

The Hague Trials began on Tuesday September 10, 2013 for Mr. William Ruto and is expected to start on February 4, 2014 for President Uhuru Kenyatta. The other indictee who faces the same charges as Mr Ruto is former Radio Journalist with Kass FM, Joshua Sang.

I feel the bewilderment of never knowing what my case against Mr. Ruto was all about, neither will I ever know who perceived that I was a witness and attempted to come after my life. My world regarding my role as a potential ICC witness remains foggy since I never got to meet Donata. I do not know the details of the legal conflict itself and what I would be required to say in court if I were to appear at The Hague.

What I believe is that Donata wanted to contact me with regards to Mr Ruto's agent offering me land in Eldoret before the Post-Election Violence (PEV) of 2007/2008. This implies that the chaos may have been planned well before elections.

I am learning to take one day at a time. I am learning to shed off all the baggage of the past, all the things that may weigh me down and deny me the chance of moving on and realising a fulfilling future. I believe I am now safe in America and being here is just a change. To God be the glory.

I do not want to dwell on death. It is inevitable and will come anyway. I will cross that bridge when I come to it…

I have decided to consciously be aware of my surroundings and dwell on positive thoughts. I have learnt to forgive and move on. There is a whole lot of life ahead of me. I will grasp every new opportunity that comes my way. For what happened to me was just a part of my journey through life.

Who knows about tomorrow? I do not. What I know is that this story must be told! And when the birds go round the world and complete their full cycle, I shall be home.

End Notes

1. Source *Wikipedia* **What is the International Criminal Court? The International Criminal Court** ("the ICC" or "the Court") *is a permanent international court established to investigate, prosecute and try individuals accused of committing the most serious crimes of concern to the international community namely the crime of genocide, crimes against humanity, war crimes and the crime of aggression.*

The International Criminal Court (commonly referred to as the ICC or ICCt)[2] is a <u>permanent tribunal</u> to prosecute individuals for <u>genocide, crimes against humanity, war crimes, and the crime of aggression (although jurisdiction for the crime of aggression[3] will not be awakened until 2017 at the earliest).[4][5]</u>

The ICC was created by the <u>Rome Statute</u> which came into force on 1 July 2002.[6][7] The Court has established itself in <u>THE HAGUE,</u> Netherlands, but its proceedings may take place anywhere.[8] It is intended to complement existing national judicial systems, and may only exercise its jurisdiction only when national courts are unwilling or unable to investigate or prosecute such crimes.

Currently, 122 states[9] are <u>states parties</u> to the Statute of the Court, including all of South America, nearly all of Europe, most of Oceania and roughly half the countries in Africa.[10] A further 31 countries,[9] including <u>Russia</u>, have signed but not <u>ratified</u> the Rome Statute.[10] The law of treaties obliges these states to refrain from "acts which would defeat the object and purpose" of the treaty until they declare they do not intend to become a party to the treaty.[11] Three of these states—Israel, Sudan and the <u>United States</u>—have informed the UN Secretary General that they no longer intend to become states parties and, as such, have no legal *obligations arising from their former representatives' signature of the Statute.[10][12] 41 <u>United Nations member states</u>[9] have neither signed nor ratified or acceded to the Rome Statute; some of them, including <u>China</u> and <u>India</u>, are critical of the Court.[13][14] On 21 January 2009, the Palestinian National Authority formally accepted the jurisdiction of the Court.[15] On 3 April 2012, the ICC Prosecutor declared himself unable to determine that Palestine is a "state" for the purposes of the Rome Statute and referred such decision to the United Nations.[16] On 29 November 2012, the United Nations General Assembly voted in favor of recognizing Palestine as a non-member observer state.[17]*

Trial history to date[edit]

The ICC issued an arrest warrant for Omar al-Bashir of Sudan over alleged war crimes in Darfur.[23]

To date, the Prosecutor has opened investigations into eight situations in Africa: the Democratic Republic of the Congo; Uganda; the Central African Republic; Darfur, Sudan; the Republic of Kenya; the Libyan Arab Jamahiriya; the Republic of Côte d'Ivoire and Mali.[24] Of these eight, four were referred to the Court by the concerned states parties themselves (Uganda, Democratic Republic of the Congo, Central African Republic and Mali), two were referred by the United Nations Security Council (Darfur and Libya) and two were begun proprio motu by the Prosecutor (Kenya and Côte d'Ivoire[25]). Additionally, by Power of Attorney from the Union of the Comoros, a law firm referred the situation on the Comorian-flagged MV Mavi Marmara vessel to the Court, prompting the Prosecutor to initiate a preliminary examination.

The Court's Pre-Trial Chambers have publicly indicted 30 people, proceedings against 23 of whom are ongoing. The ICC has issued arrest warrants for 21 individuals and summonses to nine others. Five individuals are in custody; one of them has been found guilty and sentenced (with an appeal lodged), three are being tried and one's confirmation of charges hearing has yet to begin. One individual has been acquitted and released (with an appeal lodged). Nine individuals remain at large as fugitives (although one is reported to have died). Additionally, three individuals have been arrested by national authorities, but have not yet been transferred to the Court. Proceedings against seven individuals have finished following the death of two, the dismissal of charges against another four and the withdrawal of charges against one.

As of June 2013, the Court's first trial, the Lubanga trial in the situation of the DR Congo, is in the appeals phase after the accused was found guilty and sentenced to 14 years in prison and a reparations regime was established. The Katanga-Chui trial regarding the DR Congo was concluded in May 2012; Mr Ngudjolo Chui was acquitted and released. The Prosecutor has appealed the acquittal. The decision regarding Mr Katanga is pending. The Bemba trial regarding the Central African Republic is ongoing with the defence presenting its evidence. A fourth trial chamber, for the Banda-Jerbo trial in the situation of Darfur, Sudan, has been established with the trial scheduled to begin in May 2014. There are a fifth and a sixth trial scheduled to begin in September and in November 2013 respectively in the Kenya situation, namely the Ruto-Sang and the Kenyatta trials. The decision on the confirmation of charges in the Laurent Gbagbo case in the Côte d'Ivoire situation is pending after hearings took place in February 2013 and after the decision was adjourned to give the Prosecutor more time to present compelling evidence. The confirmation of charges hearing in the Ntaganda case in the DR Congo situation is scheduled to begin in September 2013.

End note Source Wikipedia; So far, the International Criminal Court has opened investigations into eight situations in Africa: the

Democratic Republic of the Congo; Uganda; the Central African Republic; Darfur, Sudan; the Republic of Kenya; the Libyan Arab Jamahiriya; the Republic of Côte d'Ivoire and Mali.[1] Of these eight, four were referred to the Court by the concerned states parties themselves (Uganda, Democratic Republic of the Congo, Central African Republic and Mali), two were referred by the United Nations Security Council (Darfur and Libya) and two were begun proprio motu by the Prosecutor (Kenya and Côte d'Ivoire[2]). Additionally, by Power of Attorney from the Union of the Comoros, a law firm referred the situation on the Comorian-flagged MV Mavi Marmara vessel to the Court, prompting the Prosecutor to initiate a preliminary examination.

The Court publicly indicted 30 people, proceedings against 23 of whom are ongoing. The ICC has issued arrest warrants for 21 individuals and summonses to nine others. Five individuals are in custody; one of them has been found guilty and sentenced (with an appeal lodged), three are being tried and one's confirmation of charges hearing has yet to begin. One individual has been acquitted and released (with an appeal lodged). Nine individuals remain at large as fugitives (although one is reported to have died). Additionally, three individuals have been arrested by national authorities, but have not yet been transferred to the Court. Proceedings against seven individuals have finished following the death of two, the dismissal of charges against another four and the withdrawal of charges against one.

As of end September 2010, the Office of the Prosecutor had received 8,874 communications about alleged crimes. After initial review, 4,002 of these communications were dismissed as "manifestly outside the jurisdiction of the Court".[3]

2. End note: There are approximately 42 tribes in Kenya as follows: Ameru, Embu, Kalenjin, Kamba, Kikuyu, Kisii, Kuria,

Luhya, Luo, Maasai, Mijikenda, Orma, Rendille, Samburu, Somali, Suba, Swahili, Taita, Taveta, Turkana, Gabra, Mbeene, Nubi, Tharaka, Ilchamus, Njemps, Borana, Galla, Gosha, Konso, Sakuye, Waat, Isaak, Walwana, Dasenaach. Waljeel, Leysan, Bulji, Teso, Kenyan Arabs, Kenyan Asians (Kenya National Bureau of Statistics 2019). *The clickable map below shows the area where each of these tribes is predominantly found.*

Source : http//www.google.com/url
Source: Kenyanview.com

3. Source **Wikipedia**: Lake Victoria (Nam Lolwe in Luo; Victoria Nyanza in Bantu[1]) is one of the African Great Lakes. The lake was named after Queen Victoria, by John Hanning Speke, the first European to discover this lake.

With a surface area of 68,800 square kilometers (26,600 sq mi), Lake Victoria is Africa's largest lake by area, and it is the largest tropical lake in the world. Lake Victoria is the world's 2nd largest freshwater lake by surface area; only Lake Superior in North America is larger. In terms of its volume, Lake Victoria is the world's ninth largest continental lake, and it contains about 2,750 cubic kilometers (2.2 billion acre-feet) of water.

Lake Victoria receives its water primarily from direct precipitation and thousands of small streams. The largest stream flowing into this lake is the Kagera River, the mouth of which lies on the lake's western shore. Two rivers leave the lake, the White Nile (known as the "Victoria Nile" as it leaves the lake), flows out at Jinja, Uganda on the lake's north shore, and the Katonga River flows out at Lukaya on the western shore connecting the lake to Lake George. [2]

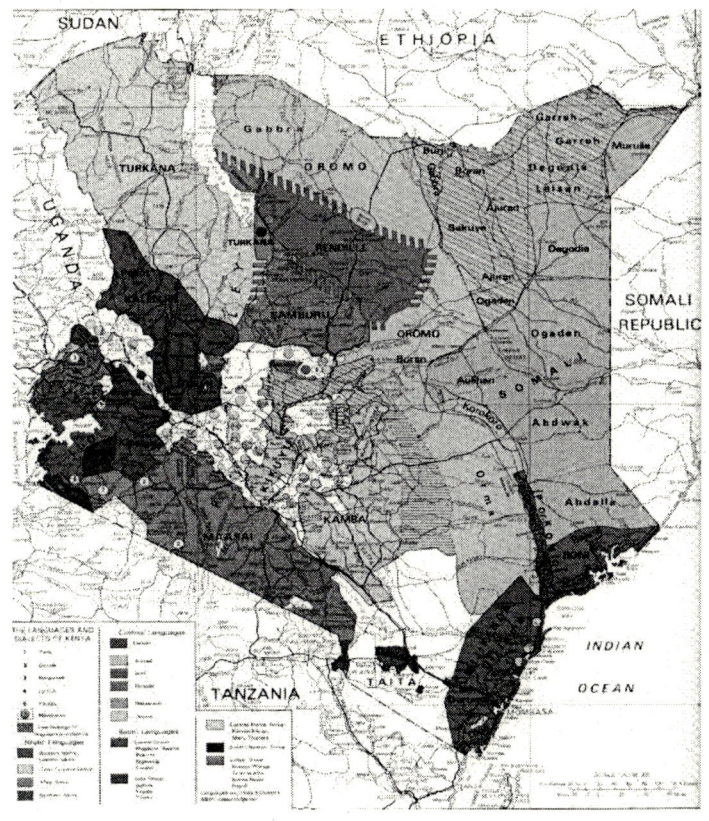

Lake Victoria occupies a shallow depression in Africa and has a maximum depth of 84 m (276 ft) and an average depth of 40 m (130 ft).[3] Its catchment area covers 184,000 square kilometers (71,040 sq mi). The lake has a shoreline of 4,828 km (3,000 mi), with islands constituting 3.7% of this length,[4] and is divided among three countries: Kenya (6% or 4,100 km2 or 1,600 sq mi), Uganda (45% or 31,000 km2 or 12,000 sq mi) and Tanzania (49% or 33,700 km 2 or 4.

Footnote: *Source Wikipedia: Mwai Kibaki, C.G.H. (born 15 November 1931) is a Kenyan politician. He was the third President of Kenya, serving from December 2002 to April 2013.*

Kibaki was first elected President in 2002 after beating Uhuru Kenyatta, now his successor as Kenya's Current and 4th President and the son of Kenya's first President, Jomo Kenyatta. Kibaki was re-elected in controversial circumstances in 2007 after beating prominent opposition leader Raila Odinga.

Kibaki was previously Vice-President of Kenya for ten years from 1978 to 1988 under President Daniel Arap Moi. He also held cabinet ministerial positions in the Kenyatta and Moi governments, including a widely-acclaimed stint as Minister for Finance (1969–1981) under Kenyatta, and Minister for Home Affairs (1982–1988) and Minister for Health (1988–1991) under Moi.[2]

Kibaki also served as an opposition Member of Parliament from 1992 up to his election in 2002 after his two unsuccessful bids for the presidency in 1992 and 1997.

5 **Footnote***: Source Wikipedia: Najib Balala (born 20 September 1967) is a Kenyan politician and former Minister for Tourism,[citation needed] and the immediate former M.P. for Mvita Constituency.[citation needed] Balala is the party leader of The Republican Congress Party of Kenya (RC), a partner of the Jubilee Coalition.*

Najib Balala the attended Serani Primary School, a Boys only day school, where he qualified to join Kakamega High, a national school [citation needed]. He studied Business Administration and International Urban Management and Leadership from the University of Toronto and the John F. Kennedy School of Government at Harvard. [citation needed]

Footnote: Najib Balala: Source: omwaombara@wordpress.com:

This Man, Najib Balala

From those early days as a young man, he stood to be conspicuous wherever he went; even as a person he has a very pleasant personality. He is handsome (what the local community called a "natural attractiveness"). He has never been a fundamentalist - he is a moderate, educated and westernized person. Even when other Arabs were being sent to local schools, his family took him to Kakamega High School. He later went to Harvard University.

At Kakamega High School, Balala related well with the institution members that were not Muslim. This is not to say that he has not been loyal to his faith. He drives his inspiration from his beads. Balala speaks fluent Luhya and loves chicken. Although his favorite food is Biryani, he has had to go slow on the dish since it is quite fattening. The former Ag. Labor Minister has special praise, almost awe when he speaks about his old school. One cannot mistake his nostalgia. "Kakamega High School taught me to be an independent thinker. To appreciate diverse cultures and understand that there is no difference in humanity, in diversity."

Najib Balala is a Monday child. He was born on an early Monday morning at Kikowani in Mombasa at the Mosque. This explains why he loves Mondays. His father died before he was born having suffered from Leukemia. He has always referred to his mother as a strong woman. "She was only 30 years and never remarried. She protected us (we were six siblings, four boys and two girls). She was a very poor woman. I am very proud of her. Her upbringing is very well cultured. Her honesty is the key to our upbringing," he told the writer in a past interview. Balala is the last born of his mother. Being poor and fatherless always inspired him to work hard and change society. He is a down to earth person who drives himself around even though he has access to a driver.

Balala is a family man and rather proud of his family. "After work, I sit with my children. If I don't give them time, they will lose personal touch. My timing is unpredictable due to the nature of my political work so I spend quality time with my family," he said.

He first cut his teeth is politics as Mombasa mayor and later as Mvita Member of Parliament and Minister for Tourism. From the start, his family was against his joining politics and he struggled alone.

His mantra is the need to start developing leadership that is honest and trustworthy and to have a mechanism to block leaders who take advantage of communities because they are more vulnerable and who think they can buy people. His greatest achievement is in the tourism sector where he introduced tourism as part of Corporate Responsibility and turned the economic sector around. He has never ceased to be a darling of the media since he always gives interviews without a fuss and always picks his calls even in the middle of a meeting.

He is highly respected within the Muslim community and never misses a function at the Mosque. Balala is accepted among Muslims who are rich, poor and middle class and by non-Muslims who are also of the same status. He is also said to be a darling with women who are the majority voters at the Coast. Before his sacking a few days ago, he was a bosom buddy of Kenya's Prime Minister, Raila Odinga until recently when they started following different political paths. He once described Raila as the only person who seemed to fight for the rights of Muslims.

6. Source: **Wikipedia**:
William Kipchirchir Samoei arap Ruto (born 21 December 1966) is a Kenyan politician and the first Deputy President of Kenya in the new Constitution. He was sworn in on 9 April 2013. He was the running mate in the successful Jubilee coalition ticket led by President Uhuru Kenyatta during the 2013 general elections. He is currently an accused suspect, by the International Criminal Court (ICC) for committing crimes against humanity. On 19

October 2010, he was suspended by the government on corruption charges. He had previously served in the Ministry of Agriculture since April 2008. Ruto was elected Director of Elections on 18 March 2002, when the National Development Party led by Raila Odinga merged with the Kenya African National Union (KANU). He was Secretary General of KANU, the former ruling political party, and he has been MP for Eldoret North Constituency since the 1997 Kenyan election, a seat he won after trouncing the former M.P. The Late Hon. Rueben Chesire. He became an Assistant Minister in the Office of the President and was appointed Minister in charge of Home Affairs in August 2002 but lost the post after the December 2002 election, in which Kenya African National Union lost to the National Rainbow Coalition. He also previously served as the Chairman of the Parliamentary Select Committee on Constitutional Reform in the 9th Parliament.

Ruto has been mentioned as orchestrating the 2007/2008 post-election violence in Kenya.[1] On 3 November 2010, Ruto flew to the International Criminal Court at The Hague to discuss an evidence deal with the prosecutor. On 15 December 2010, Ruto was named in a summon by the prosecutor of the International Criminal Court, Luis Moreno-Ocampo, in relation to his alleged role in violence which followed the 2007 elections.

Questions and Exercises for Discussion

1. Do You Think "God's Child on The Run" is a good title for the Book? If yes, why/ If no, why? What title would you give the book if you were the author?

2. Discuss conflict in the book. How does the conflict develop or enhance the theme?

3. How does the setting affect the conflict?

4. The author talks about trails of injustices. Can you identify at least 3 such cases?

5. Explore some of the major themes in this story. What do you think the author wants you to learn in this story?

6. Discuss the theme of corruption in the book.

7. What is the central theme of the book?

8. How do some of the symbols within the story develop or enhance the theme?

9. How does the author's tone of the story develop or enhance the theme?

10. How does the setting affect the plot?

11. Identify some of the imagery, similes and metaphors the author uses to develop her story.

12. Discuss the protagonist's flaws or weaknesses.

13. What motivates the protagonist to act?

14. What are your favorite quotes in the book? Name at least 3.

15. Give 3 examples of dramatization in the book.

16. The author's best friend tells her to go and look for her mother when she seeks her help. Should she have hidden her in her house? Discuss.

17. A flashback is a scene that you show in your story in real time, but which happened in the past. Identify some of the flashbacks the author uses in the story. Do they effectively fill the gaps in the story or do they derail and slow down the plot?

18. Explore the use of irony, hyperbole, satire, dialect, comic relief and humor as literary tools in God's Child on The Run (Revisited)

19. A Fable in Literature describes a didactic lesson given through some sort of animal story. In prose and verse, a fable is described through plants, animals, forces of nature and inanimate objects by giving them human attributes wherein they demonstrate a moral lesson at the end. Identify the didactic role of fables in the story.

20. How does the author depict the women in her story? What about the men?

21. What are some of the writer's childhood memories you enjoyed reading the most? Which ones reminded you of your own childhood?

22. Imagine you bing the writer. Consider your network of friends, family and relatives,. Where would you seek refuge in the wake of this kind of danger?

23. If you met the writer today, what are some of the questions you would ask her?

24. Would you abandon your life and everything you do today to be a witness? If yes, why? If no, why?

Biography

OMWA OMBARA is a Writing Consultant, political Asylee, Protest Poet and a widely travelled international investigative journalist. She is the Co-Founder and Editor-In-Chief at Tujipange Africa Media, a Diaspora E-Magazine (an e-magazine that provides the latest News, Features, Resources and Entertainment from Kenya and Diaspora). She has over 20-year experience in the media and was the first woman bureau chief in 104 years of existence of the Standard Group in East Africa.

She holds a postgraduate diploma in journalism and mass communication and a BA degree, both from the University of Nairobi, Kenya.

As a Publisher, she founded 'Aids Digest' monthly magazine in 2008 and Maisha Save a Breast Cancer Annual Dinner Dance Fundraiser in 2004.

Her writing career started in 1989 with her published poem 'Holding the Centre' and her story, "The Wedding," in the Anthology, "Our Secret Lives".

Omwa Ombara also co-hosts an online Saturday Diaspora Breakfast Live Show, "Kumechacha" (Crossfire) with Grace and Grace. She currently volunteers as an Editor with Safari Yangu, New York office.